20 tunings

CHORDS TUNINGS SCALES

CHARTS

Jan Mohr / Robert Klein

Voggenreiter

Cover design: OZ, Essen (Christian & Katrin Brackmann)
Setting-up and Layout: B & O

VOGGENREITER PUBLISHERS
Viktoriastraße 25, D-53173 Bonn/Germany
www.voggenreiter.de
Phone: +(49) 228-93 575-0

Revised Edition 2008

ISBN: 978-3-8024-0397-2

Foreword

Open or alternate tunings are a favored way of widening the variety of musical expression for many guitarists. Right across all styles of playing, changing the pitch of the guitar is extremely popular. Joni Mitchell, Stanley Jordan, George van Eps, Ry Cooder, Duane Allmann, Albert Collins, Edward van Halen, Diamond Darrell ... this list of famous guitarists who retune their guitars (some more, some less) could easily be added to.

In this book, we have tried to present the most popular alternate tunings. This compilation does not lay claim to being complete (during one concert alone Joni Mitchell uses a greater variety of tunings than is listed here!). So we hope you will understand that not everybody's "favorite tuning" can be included here. Given the immense number of theoretical possibilities of retuning the guitar (and each day brings new ones), we thought it more important to describe the best-known tunings and explain how they are used, so that the information given here can be put into practice immediately. All tunings are presented in the same way:

1) A chart shows which strings have to be retuned and where the respective notes required are to be found.
2) A short explanation gives information on the background and use of the tuning in question. This information is of course not obligatory, but merely provides rough guidelines.
3) On the second and third page of each open tuning fingering diagrams for certain selected chords are given.
4) The conclusion shows the most important scales of the tuning concerned. They are shown here both in traditional notation as well as in tablature form.

The Appendix of this book contains further information:

- Transposition and capo table in order to transpose the chords, scales and tunings as required.
- Basic chords for standard tuning.
- Summary and explanation listing the most common symbols used for chords.

Have fun!

CONTENTS

Tunings in C

Other Tunings

Special Forms of Changing the Tuning

Appendix

Introduction

Tuning Charts

In this book we use diagrams to illustrate the pitch of the individual retuned strings. The desired pitch of the open (unfingered) string is shown on the left of the specific chart. At the same time these charts contain information as to which string has to be retuned.

As always there is also one exception here: for all tunings that require a retuning of the low E string, we have indicated this with a small arrow to the left of the name of the note. If it points downwards, the low E string has to be tuned lower, should it be tuned higher, the arrow points upwards. Here is an example of **Open D** tuning:

This chart reads as follows:

In order to retune the guitar to Open D, the strings must be tuned to D A D F♯ A D (from the low to the high E string). Here the low E string is tuned down to D. Next the open A is tuned to the note on the 7th fret of the E string (now with the pitch of D), then the D string to the 5th fret of the A string, the G string to the 4th fret of the D

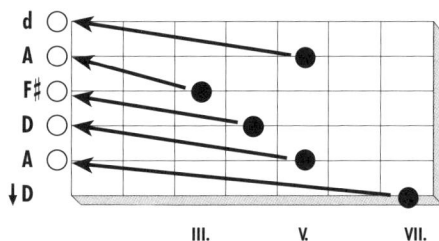

string, etc. up to the high E string. The notes, following the successful retuning process, are shown to the left of the chart.

Note: Presuming that the guitar was perfectly tuned right from the start, the A and D strings can of course be left unchanged, as their pitch is not changed compared to standard tuning.

To avoid confusion, the names of the strings are always quoted in this book in the standard tuning. When talking about the "low E string", we mean the lowest (thickest) string of the guitar, no matter to which note this string has been retuned in one particular tuning.

Chord Charts

We have presented the most important chords of each tuning in the international-ly accepted chart form to make the first steps in open tunings as easy as possible. Naturally there are thousands of interesting chords which sound good in each open tuning (just as in standard tuning). One of the most fascinating challenges is to discover more ...

In the chord charts, the horizontal lines represent the strings, the vertical ones the frets.

The fingers of the playing hand are numbered:

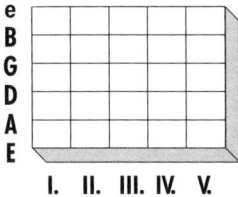

1 = Index finger
2 = Middle finger
3 = Ring finger
4 = Little Finger

Open strings to be plucked when playing a chord are marked with a circle "o" on the left of the chart; strings which should not be played with an "x".

If a chord is not played on the first, but on a higher fret, the corresponding positi-on is described more closely underneath the chart.

The following chart for a C Major 7th chord (in standard tuning to make it easier) denotes:

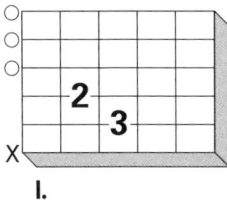

The low E string is damped, i.e. not played
The 3rd finger plays the A string on the 3rd fret,
the 2nd finger plays the D string on the 2nd fret.
The G, B and high E strings – open strings - are
also played.

Note: In many open tunings particularly beautiful voicings can only be played if the left thumb is wrapped around the neck. This way of holding the instrument – for classical players considered "incorrect" – is deliberately called for here.

Scale Charts

As in the case of the chord charts for the individual tunings, our brief scale summary is not aimed at dealing in detail with the subject of "Scales in Open Tunings", but at providing the motivated guitarist with quick access to playing these scales.

For this reason we have selected the following:

- major scales
- (natural) minor scales,
- major Pentatonic
- and minor Pentatonic.

All these scales are illustrated in notes and tablature with a range of two octaves. As tonic note we have chosen the respective tonic of the open tuning. By moving along the guitar fretboard, the scales can be transposed into different keys. For example, to play a G minor scale instead of an A minor scale, simply play the pattern shown two frets lower.

We have purposely dispensed with showing all possible patterns for each scale, as, depending on the desired effect, there are innumerable patterns for each scale, which confuse rather than stimulate immediate playing. From the first pattern, the others are easily derived, with a little practice, for each scale ...

The **Basic Principle** is as follows:

The first pattern of the scale begins with the root on the low E string, the second pattern begins with the second scale note of the scale on the low E string, etc. When the scale fingering is established according to this system (there are a large number of other systems), there are just as many patterns for each scale as the number of notes in the scale. A normal major or minor scale has seven patterns, a major or minor pentatonic has only five.

In the example on the next page we have shown all five patterns of an A minor pentatonic in standard tuning. To illustrate the principle, the chart shows the same in graphic form (here the tonic of the scale is set off in white).

Pattern of the A minor Pentatonic in Standard tuning

1. Pattern

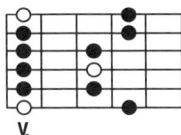

2. Pattern

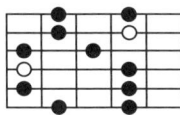

3. Pattern

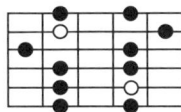

4. Pattern

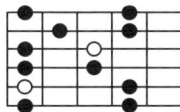

5. Pattern

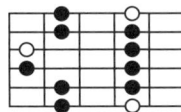

By practising the scales simply up and down, a certain familiarity with the sound and fingering of the scales will be gained, thus opening up many other creative ways of practicing scales, all of which can be found in the relevant literature and are not dealt with here.

On fingering: In principle, the following rule applies: "one finger per fret"

Unfortunately in the case of Open Tunings, this principle cannot always be adhered to. The best fingering here depends very much on individual circumstances such as the size and span of the hand; so be bold and experiment!

Open E

This is (together with Open D) probably the most popular open tuning. The guitar is tuned so that its open strings produce an E major chord. By playing a simple barre on all six strings other major chords can be played very easily. Extensions of the major chords with sevenths and ninths are also easy to play.

Minor chords and their extensions are, however, a little more difficult. Bottle-neck guitarists in particular like to use this tuning (just like open G).

Many blues guitarists of the older generation have also used open E in order to achieve a really full sound. Furthermore with very little playing technique, some wonderful "exotic" chords can be produced, which in standard tuning are very difficult or not playable at all; so by all means try and experiment ...

This tuning provides another good effect:
The most important chords of the key of E major can be played completely as **harmonics** by simply placing the index finger on the 5th, 7th or 12th fret loosely over all six strings and after playing, lifting it immediately from the strings.

Note: Depending on the guitar being used, it could be advisable to change to a lighter gauge of string, as for Open E a total of three strings have to be tuned up, which significantly increases the tension placed on the neck.

Open E is used above all in blues and related styles of music. Musicians and bands who have recorded in Open E include: Allmann Brothers, Rory Block, Eric Clapton, Ry Cooder, Alex deGrassi, John Fahey, John Hammond, Robert Johnson, Roy Rogers and George Thorogood.

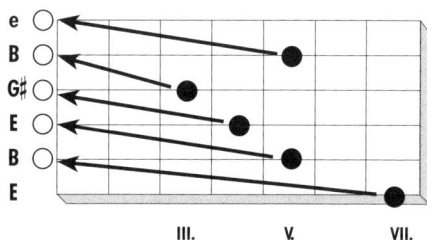

E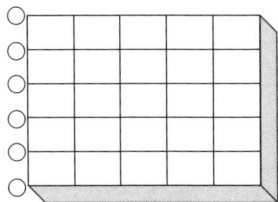

A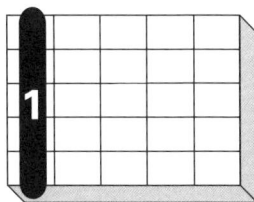
V.

E^{maj7}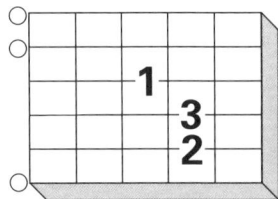

E^{maj7}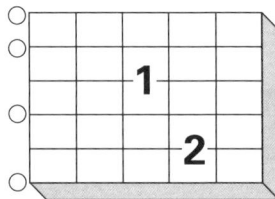

A^{add9}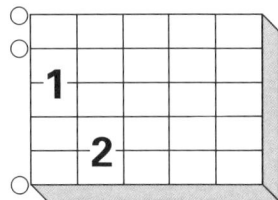

A⁷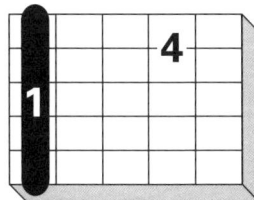
V.

F♯m¹¹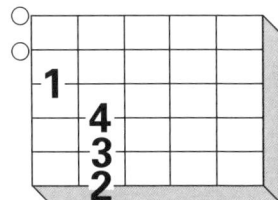

B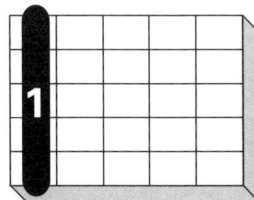
VII.

B^{add4}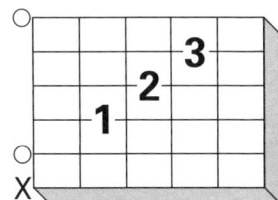

B⁷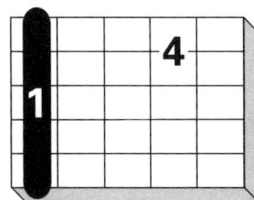
VII.

Open E

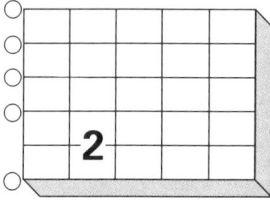

E^6

B♭^{7}

VI.

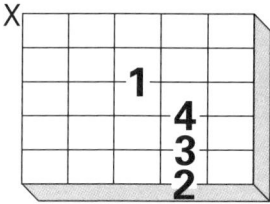

G#m

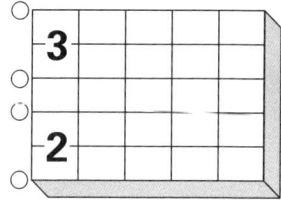

E^{add9}

VII.

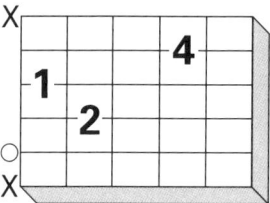

B^7

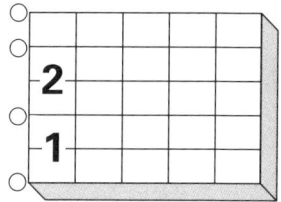

Am^9

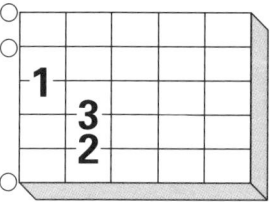

A$^{6/9}$

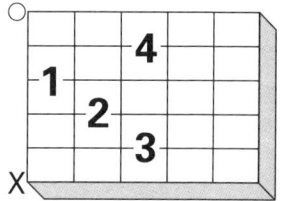

D^{add9}

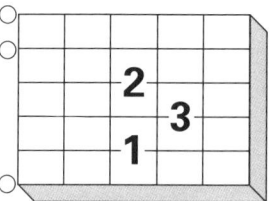

E^7

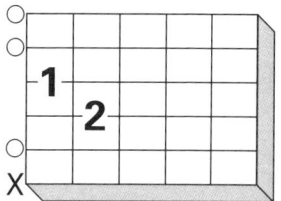

B^{7sus4}

E Major scale

E Minor scale

E Major pentatonic

E Minor pentatonic

Open Em

This is a rather rare tuning. Open D minor and Open E minor are related to each other in a similar way as Open D to Open E:
The second tuning is simply a variation on the first – tuned a whole-step higher – although many musicians prefer the lower tuned version on account of its particularly full sound.

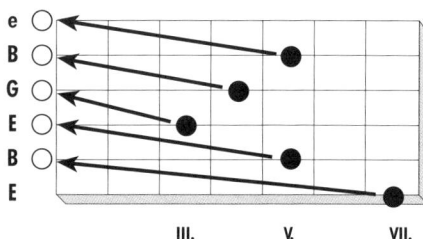

A variation of this tuning is the so-called Em7 tuning (E B D G B E)

The blues musician Skip James often used an Open E minor tuning in the Thirties, among other things for the song "Hard Time Killing Floor".

E

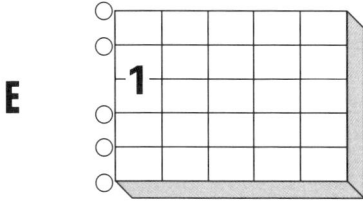

E

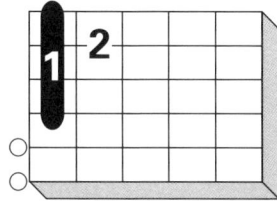

IV.

Emaj7

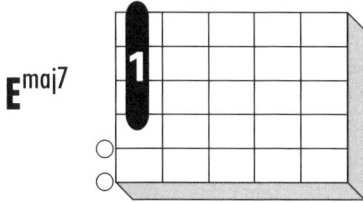

IV.

Emaj7

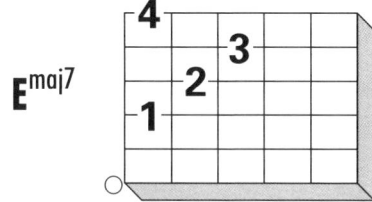

VII.

Em

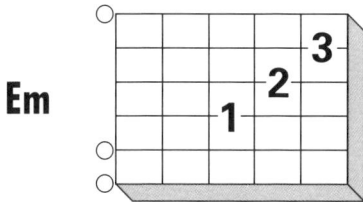

Em

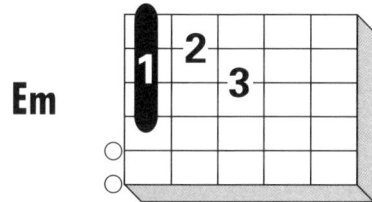

VII.

Em7

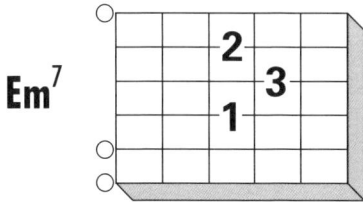

Em7

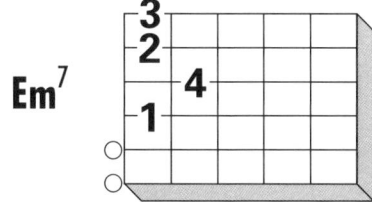

III.

B7

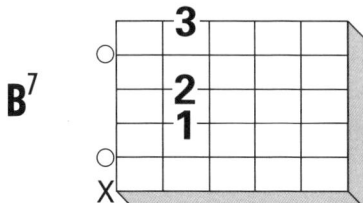

B7

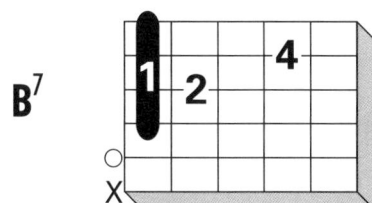

VII.

Open Em

A
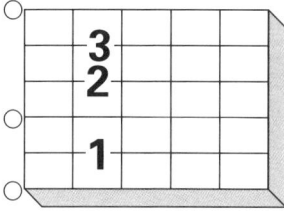

A⁶
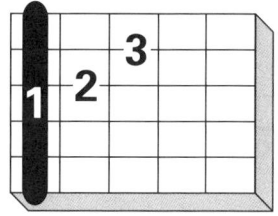
V.

A⁶
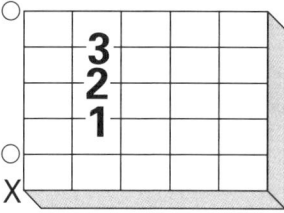

Bm
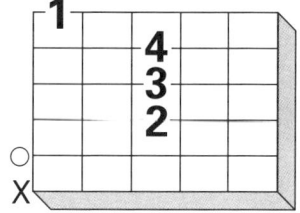
V.

B
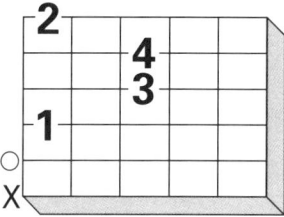
II.

E⁶
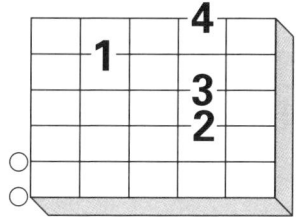

B⁷
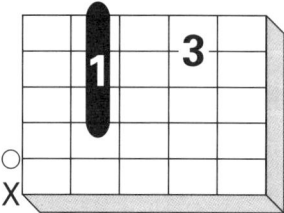

Eᵃᵈᵈ⁹
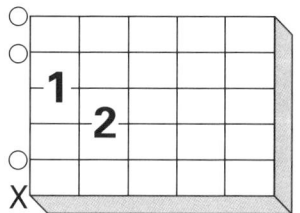

Am⁹
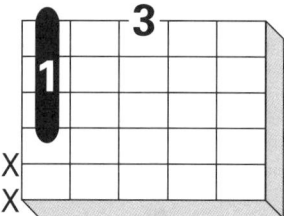
V.

Am⁷
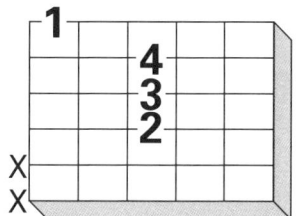
III.

E Major scale

E Minor scale

E Major pentatonic

E Minor pentatonic

Open D

This tuning is used by many blues and slide guitarists, but has also won a large number of fans in the folk and finger-style scene.

It is sometimes also described as **Vestapol** tuning (after the song with the same name).

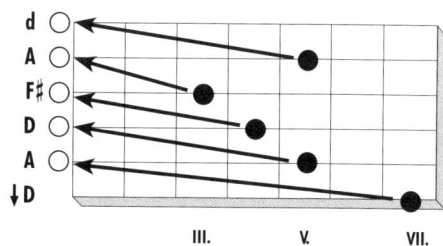

Open D is closely related to Open E (those who wish can simply imagine this tuning as Open E transposed down a whole-step), but to our ears it sounds clearly more powerful, and is thus especially suitable for solo work.
Furthermore, Open D is particularly suited to modal and pedal-point compositions, as the tonic lies on the lowest open string.

Musicians using this tuning include Jackson Browne, Joni Mitchell, Richie Havens, Ry Cooder, Jorma Kaukonen, Emmylou Harris and Harvey Reid. Open D sounds especially good on a Western guitar with heavier gauged strings (than for standard tuning). This brings out the sonorous character of this tuning.

D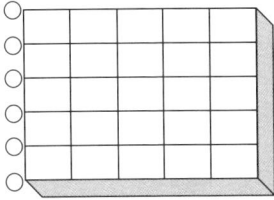

D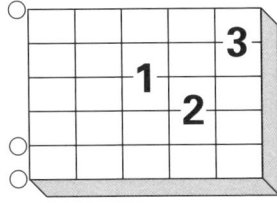

III.

Dmaj7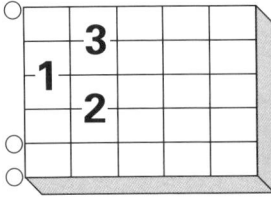

III.

Dmaj7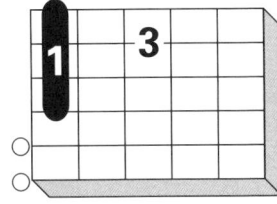

VII.

Dm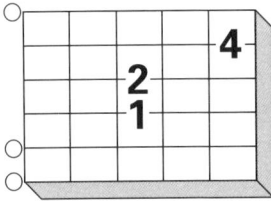

Dm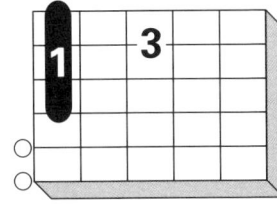

III.

Dm7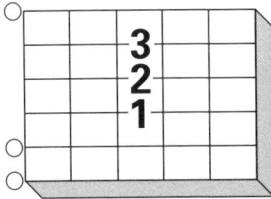

Dm7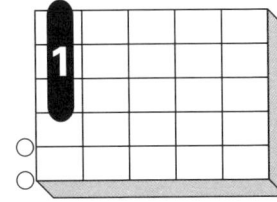

III.

A7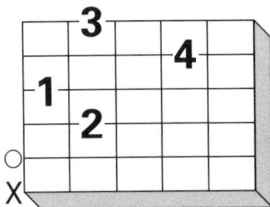

A7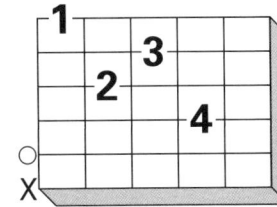

II.

Open D

G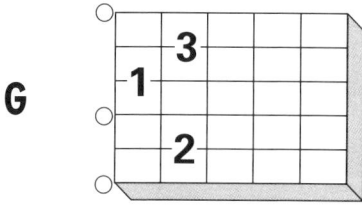

G^6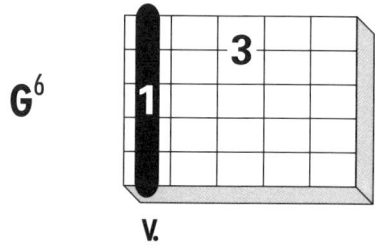

V.

Em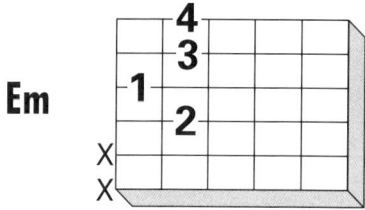

Fm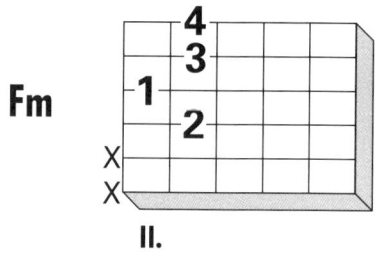

II.

Bm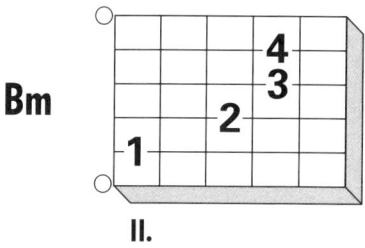

II.

D^6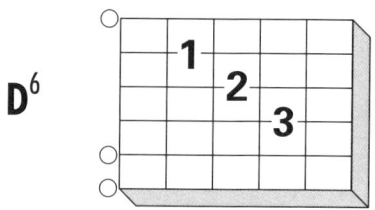

D$^{7/9}$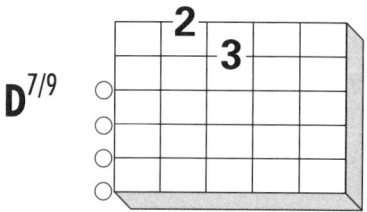

D^{sus4}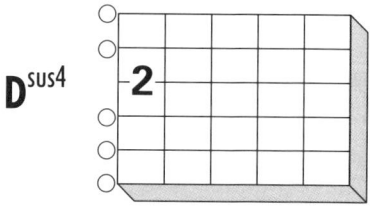

D^9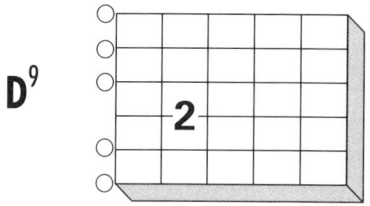

Gm^7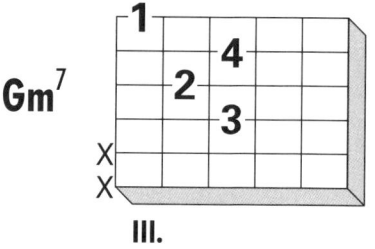

III.

D Major scale

D Minor scale

D Major pentatonic

D Minor pentatonic

Drop D

This is actually one of the easiest alternate tunings: in standard tuning, just tune the low E string down a whole step lower to D. Experienced musicians simply tune the low E string by ear an octave lower than the (open) D string.

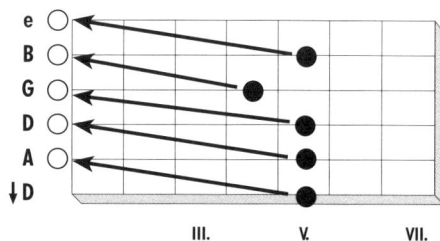

Drop D is an extremely popular tuning, often used by Ry Cooder, Stephen Stills, Leo Kottke, James Taylor and John Denver. It also enjoys great popularity with rock musicians. Drop D fans include Pearl Jam, the Beatles, Eddie van Halen and The Band.

In addition, Drop D is required for a good part of Johann Sebastian Bach's lute music. Drop D is thus one of the few alternate tunings that is also used regularly by classically trained guitarists (in classical music retuning the guitar is known as **Scordatura**).

Drop D sounds very good in all pieces of music related to the note of D: Pieces in D Major or D minor, but also chords with the root D take on a very full and sonorous sound with the retuned bass string.

One important advantage of this tuning is that many of the voicings learned in standard tuning can be used (possibly with slight adjustments).
This tuning has a close relative, the so-called Double Drop D tuning (see p.30)

A variation of this tuning is G A D G B E.

D

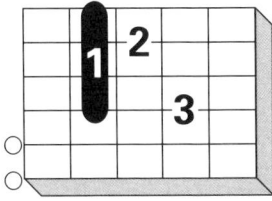

D

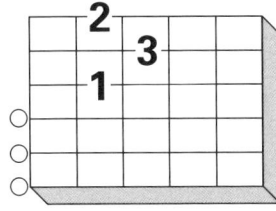

D⁷

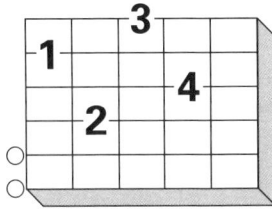

III.

Dᵐᵃʲ⁷

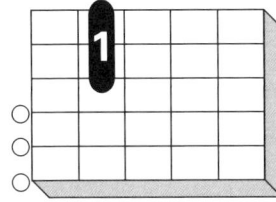

Dm

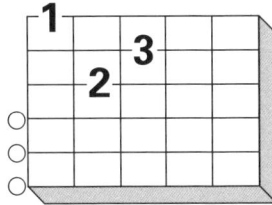

Dm

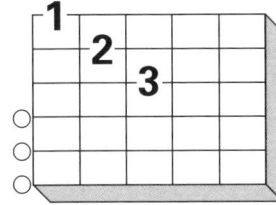

V.

Dm⁷

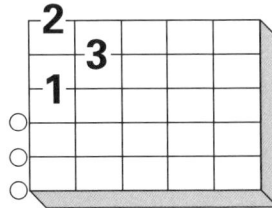

V.

Dm⁷

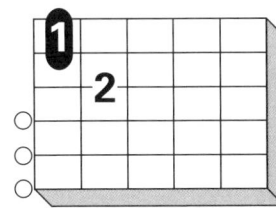

A⁷

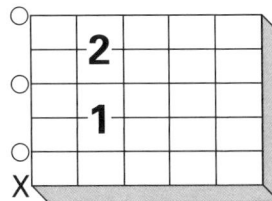

A⁹

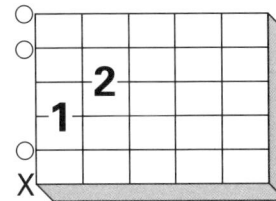

V.

Drop D

G

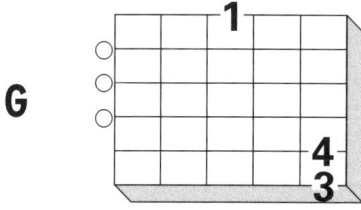

D⁹

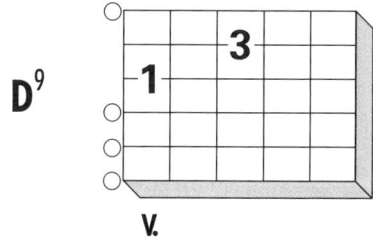

V.

Em

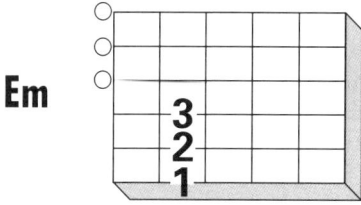

Em⁷

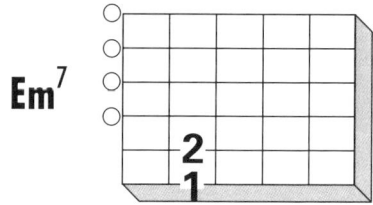

E

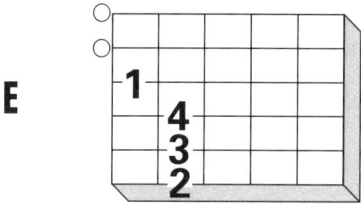

E⁷

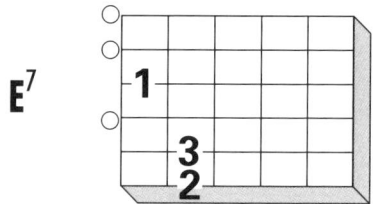

Dadd9

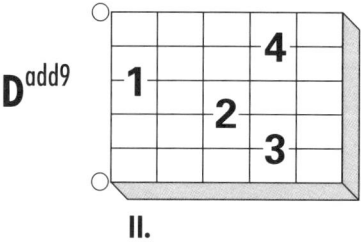

II.

D⁶

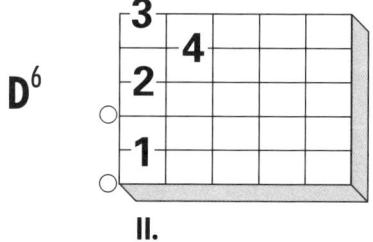

II.

Dsus4

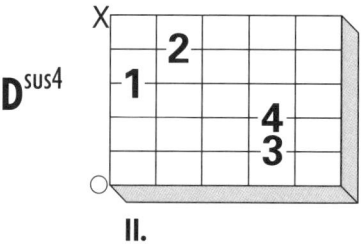

II.

Gm⁷

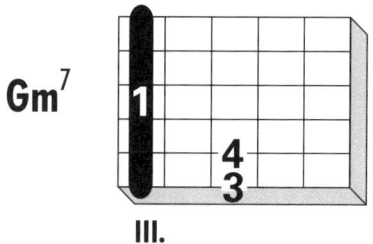

III.

D Major scale

D Minor scale

D Major pentatonic

D Minor pentatonic

Drop D2

It is noticeable in this tuning that the interval between the D and G strings is only a major second (a whole-step).

As a result, Drop D2 (as we have named this tuning) has a certain similarity with D Modal (see p. 38).

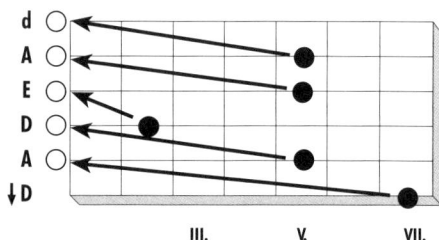

The major second interval between the strings gives this tuning a particularly flowing scale action, especially when using open strings; it is relatively easy to re-arrange the fingering shown here for this. This tuning is best found if the guitar is already tuned to open D; then only the G string needs to be tuned down a whole-step from F♯ to E.

This tuning is used by many Celtic players, and is also heard occasionally in the Country scene. The finger-style specialist John Renbourn has also written compositions for this tuning.

A variation of this tuning is D A D E A E. For this tuning, many chords and scales can be used from Drop D2, only notes on the high E string have to be played a whole step (two frets) lower.

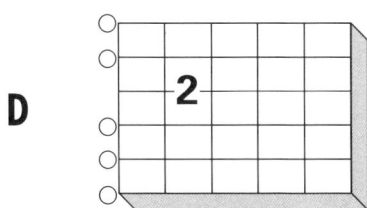

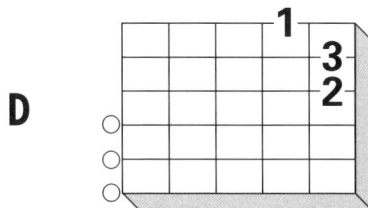

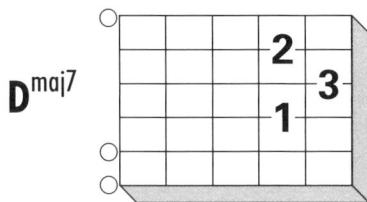

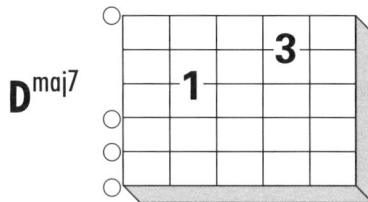

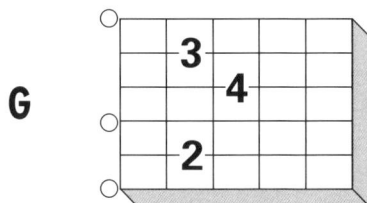

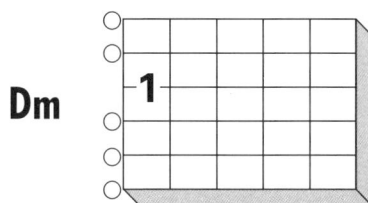

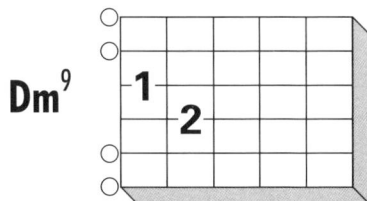

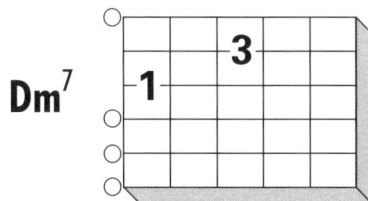

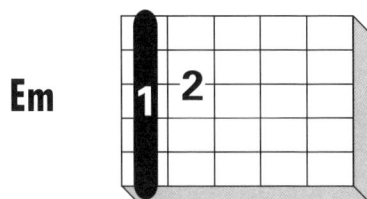

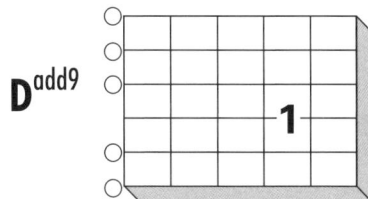

D

D

Dmaj7

Dmaj7

G

Dm

Dm9

Dm7

Em

II.

Dadd9

Drop D2

D⁷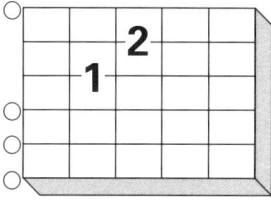

D⁹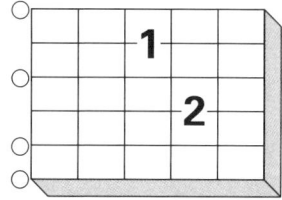

Em¹¹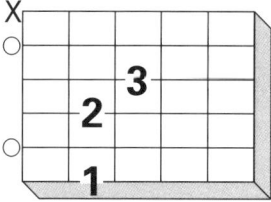

Gᵃᵈᵈ⁹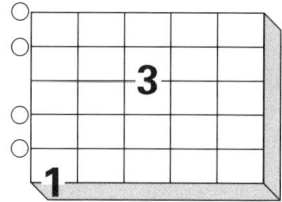

G⁶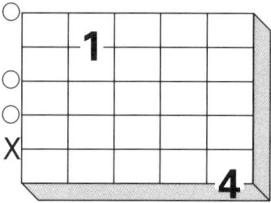

Gm⁹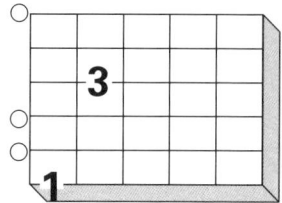

Bm⁷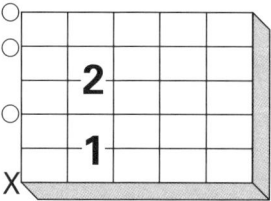

C⁶/⁹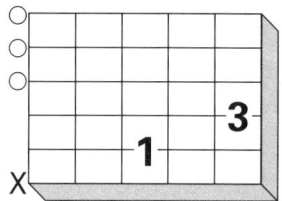

B♭ᵐᵃʲ⁷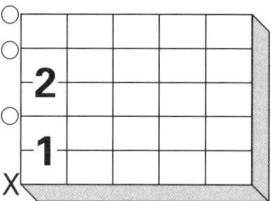

A⁷/¹¹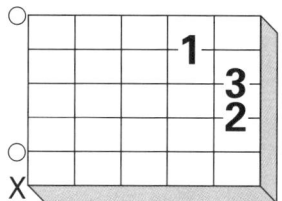

D Major scale

D Minor scale

D Major pentatonic

D Minor pentatonic

Double-Drop D

This is a variation of Drop D.
For Double Drop D, the low **and** the high E strings are tuned down to D (hence the name).

This tuning is relatively easy to obtain from standard tuning.

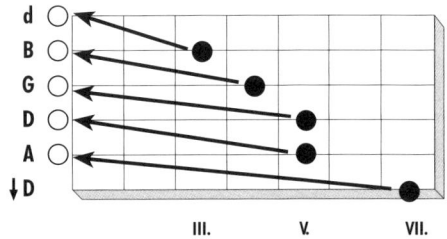

Apart from the tuning method described here, there is an alternative for musicians with a good ear; a considerably more elegant solution to tune to Double Drop D: First of all the low E string is tuned exactly an octave lower than the open D string, then the high E string is tuned two octaves higher than the low E string. With a little practice, the guitar can be retuned very quickly (even in the middle of a song). The English finger-style virtuoso Adrian Legg often uses this and similar tuning tricks.

Double Drop D is used mainly in folk music; Stephen Stills, Neil Young, John Renbourn, Adrian Legg, and Chris Proctor often play in Double Drop D. The best-known song in this tuning is probably Neil Young's "Cinnamon Girl".
In Double Drop D, the four inner strings stay in standard tuning, so that the standard chords (with slight adjustments) can be easily adopted.

The fingering of scales for Double Drop D is the same as for Drop D, with the exception of the high E string. If the scales shown here are to be extended over more than two octaves, the notes and tablature charts can be extended accordingly.

D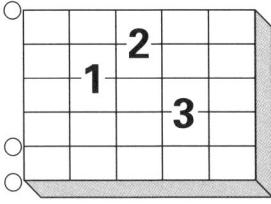

D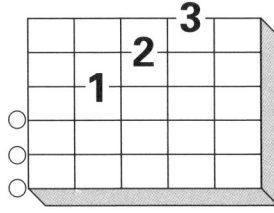

D^6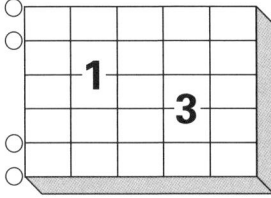

D^{maj7}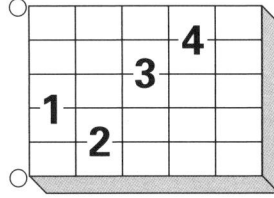

IV.

Dm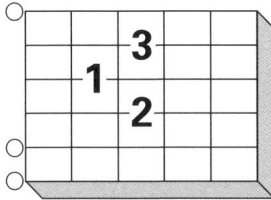

Dm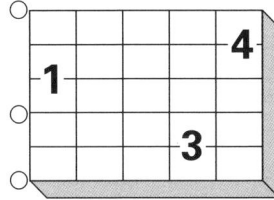

II.

E^7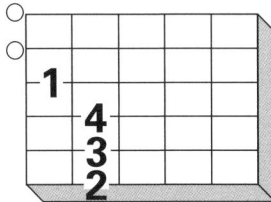

C^{maj7}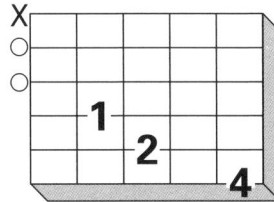

G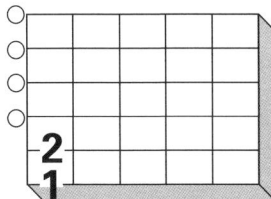

V.

G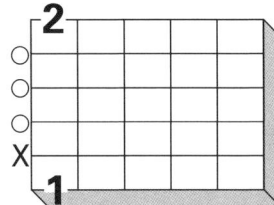

V.

Double-Drop D

D^{add11}

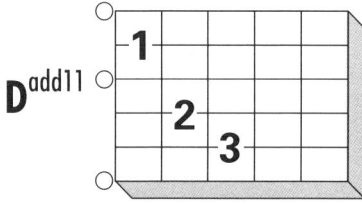

III.

G

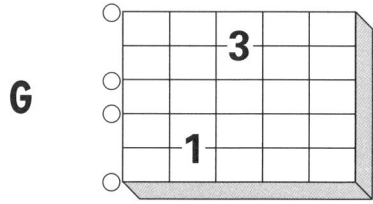

Em

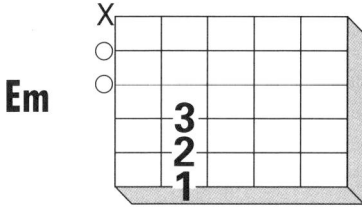

G⁶

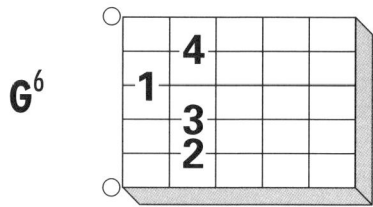

IV.

D⁷

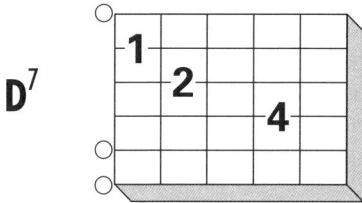

D⁷

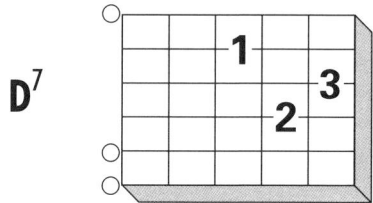

A^{add11}

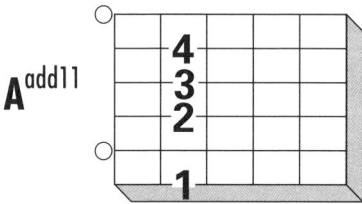

G⁷

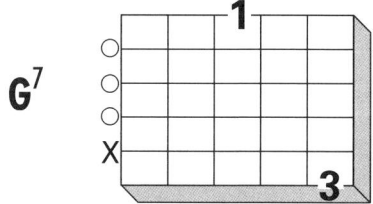

G⁷

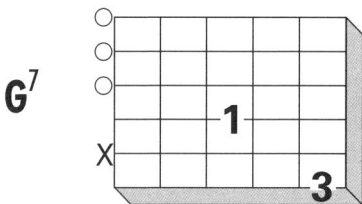

A⁷

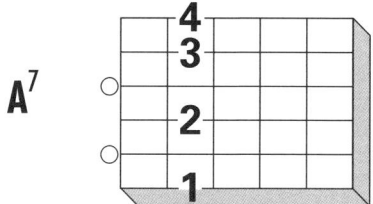

D Major scale

D Minor scale

D Major pentatonic

D Minor pentatonic

Open Dm

This tuning can be interpreted as a variation on Open D, whereby only the G string (in Open D tuned to F♯) is tuned a half-step lower.

This is a very sonorous tuning, with the tonic on the low E string, which can be used very effectively as a bass drone. Some musicians who use this tuning (both live and in the studio) include Skip James, Bukka White, The Eagles and fingerstyle guitarist Peter Finger.

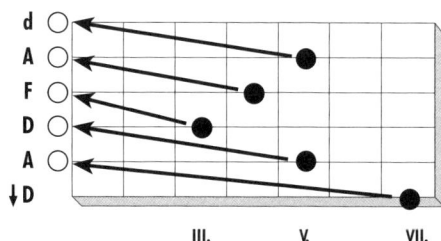

A delightful variation of this tuning is the Dm7 tuning used by Richie Havens, whereby the high E string is tuned down to C. For another variation of the Dm7 tuning, the B string is tuned up to C (D A D F C D).
This tuning also lends itself for playing natural or artificial harmonics.

Note: A big advantage of this tuning is the fact that the intervals between the three melody strings are identical with those in standard tuning. This means that all chords and scales learned on the three melody strings in standard tuning can also be used without any problem in Open Dm. With the three retuned bass strings, these chords can be extended with additional notes very effectively ...

D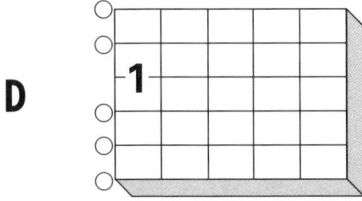

D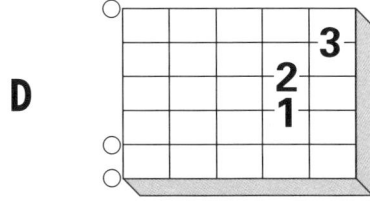

D^{maj7}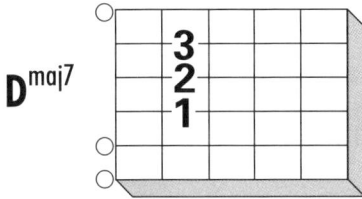

III.

D^{maj7}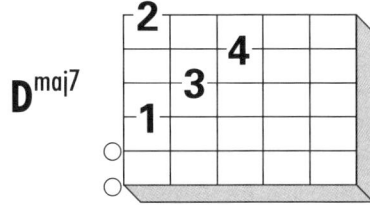

VII.

Dm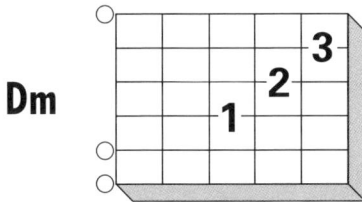

Dm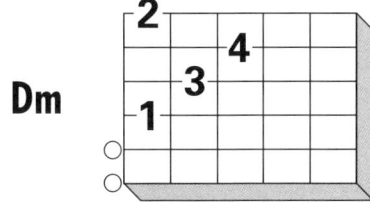

III.

Dm⁷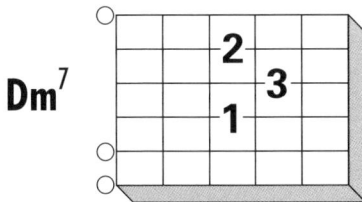

Dm⁷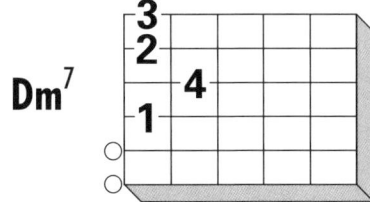

III.

A⁷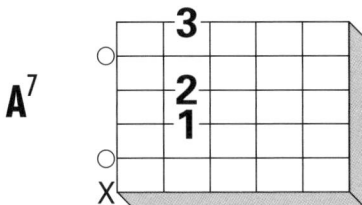

A⁷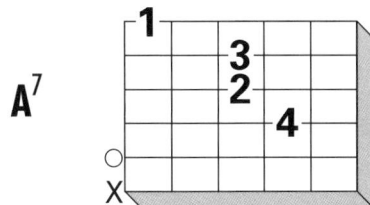

II.

Open Dm

G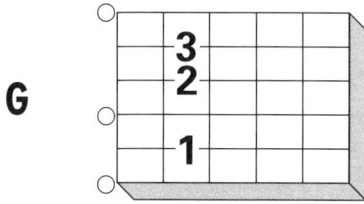

G^6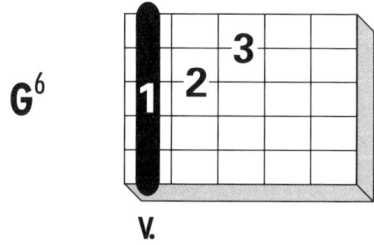
V.

Em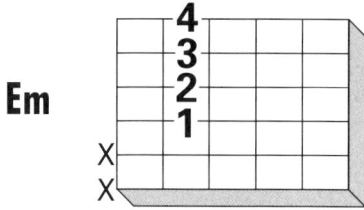

Fm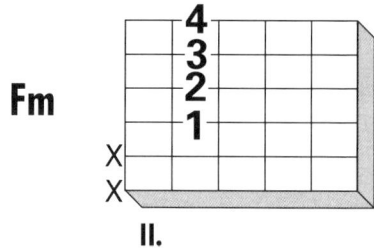
II.

B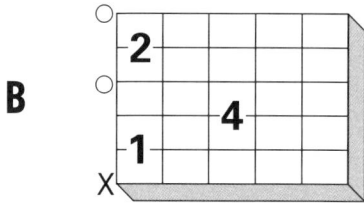

D^6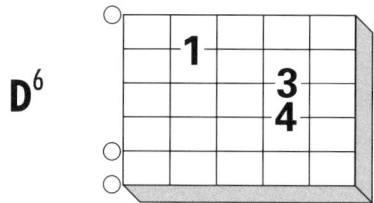

D$^{7/9}$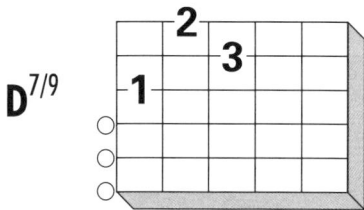

D^{sus4}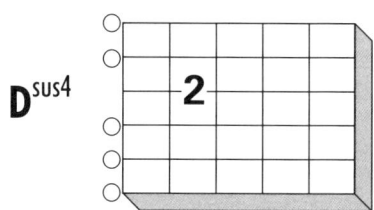

D^9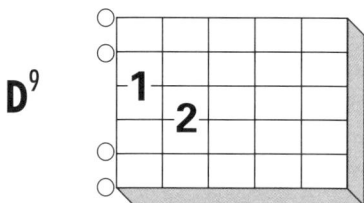

Gm^7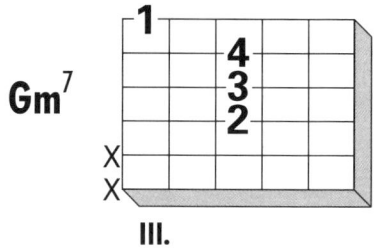
III.

D Major scale

D Minor scale

D Major pentatonic

D Minor pentatonic

D-Modal

D Modal is often also referred to as Dsus4. Both names relate to the fact that it is a tuning with the root, but lacking the third.

As the third of a chord always determines the mode (major or minor), D Modal has a certain ambiguity.

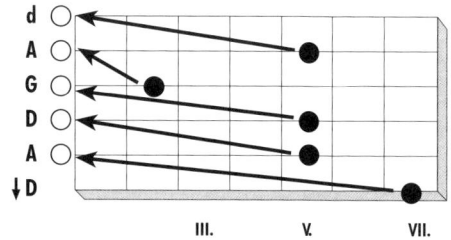

Allegedly the English guitarist, Davey Graham, returned from a visit to Morocco in the early Sixties, where he had played with the local Oud players with this tuning as it were "in his suitcase".

In England, this tuning was very quickly adopted by musicians such as John Renbourn and Bert Jansch; the best known piece in D Modal must certainly be "Black Mountain Side" by Led Zeppelin. More recently the famous guitar virtuoso, Pierre Bensusan, has used this tuning.

D Modal tuning is above all noteworthy for the interval of a second between the G and B strings. It allows two consecutive notes of the scale to be played without fretting one of them (not possible in standard tuning).

Also the resulting sound effect when the G and B strings are played simply with a small barre is extremely interesting: In this way two consecutive notes can sound together, which although not impossible in standard tuning is much more difficult to manage.

Due to this sound effect, D Modal tuning is appreciated most of all by musicians who are closely associated with traditional English and Celtic folk music, but there are, of course, also some exceptions to this rule.

D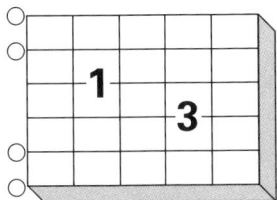

Dm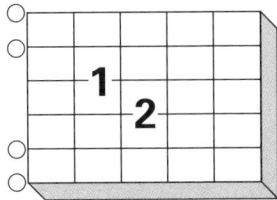

D^{maj7}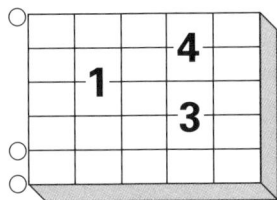

D^{maj7}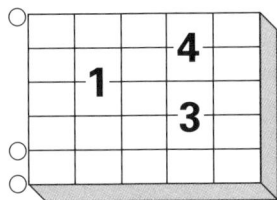

D^{11}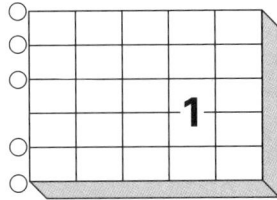

Dm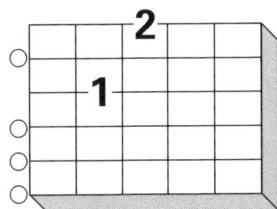

A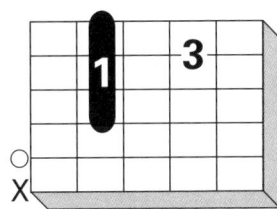

Am^{7}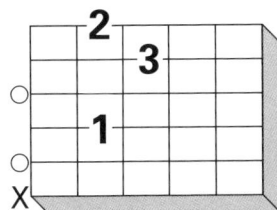

Am^{11}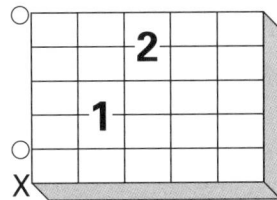

D^{7}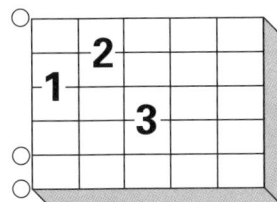

II.

A^{7}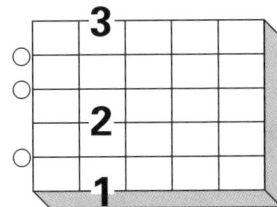

D-Modal

G
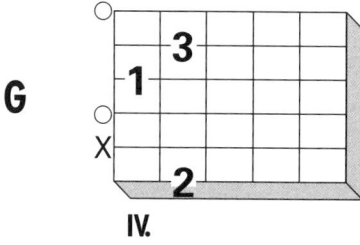
IV.

Gadd9
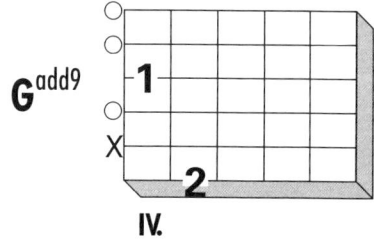
IV.

C6/9
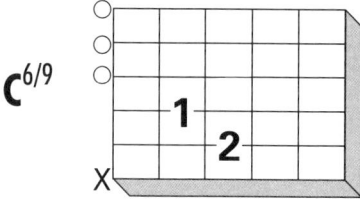

Cadd9
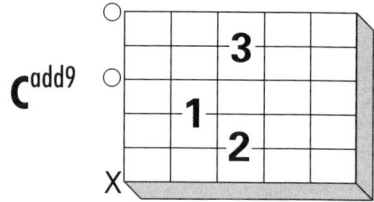

Em7
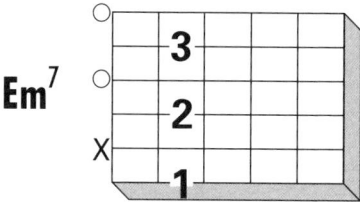

Gm
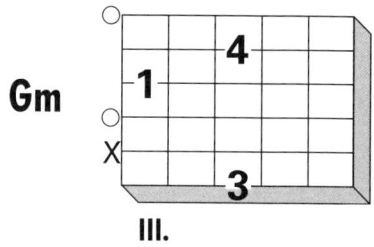
III.

Gm9
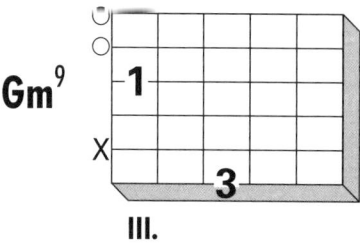
III.

D9
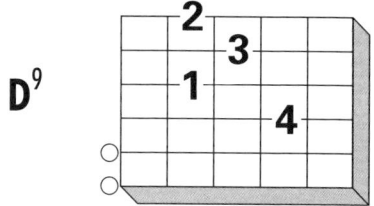

E7
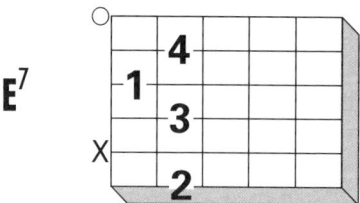

A7
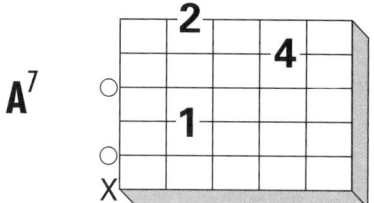

D Major scale

D Minor scale

D Major pentatonic

D Minor pentatonic

Open G

D G D G B d

This is one of the oldest open tunings, the history of which dates back to the 18th century (at least). It is occasionally referred to as **Spanish Tuning** and was popular at the beginning of the 20th century with blues guitarists.

This tuning is also often used by Hawaian Slack-Key guitarists where it is named **Taro Patch.**

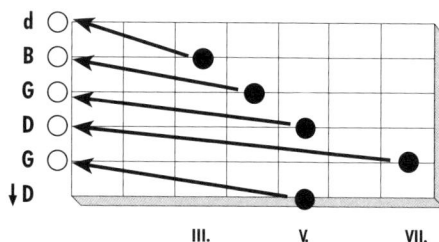

Regardless of the music style, this tuning has always been very popular with slide guitarists. It has also been used by well-known celebrities such as Eric Clapton, Peter Frampton, John Hammond, Stefan Grossmann, Jorma Kaukonen, James Taylor and many others.

In this tuning as well, there is a shorter way for experienced guitarists to retune the guitar: First of all the low E string is tuned an octave lower than the open D string, then the high E string two octaves higher than the low E string. Now the A string only has to be tuned down a whole-step – all done.

This tuning is closely related to Open D, but with one important difference: In Open D the tonic also happens to be the lowest string of the tuning, in Open G this is the fifth of the scale, whereas the lowest tonic is only to be found on the second lowest open string. For this reason Open D in direct comparison has a considerably fuller sound than Open G. As "compensation" there are some particularly beautiful chord voicings in Open G.

G

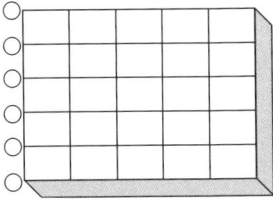

C

V.

Gmaj7

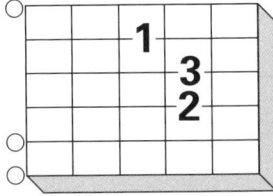

Gmaj7

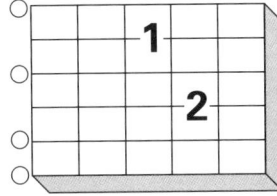

Cadd9

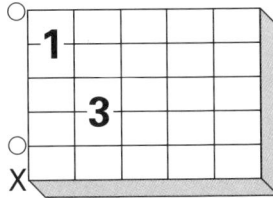

X

Cadd9

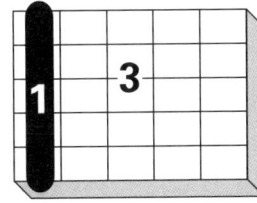

V.

C

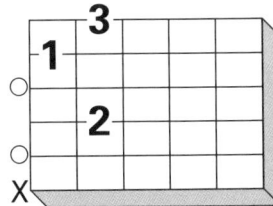

X

D

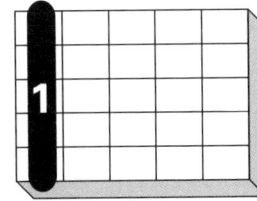

VII.

Am11

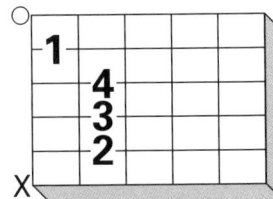

X

C7

X

V.

Open G

G^{maj7}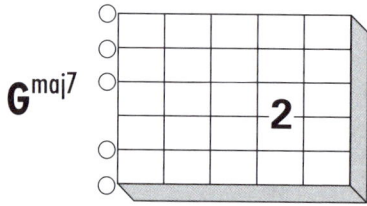

G⁷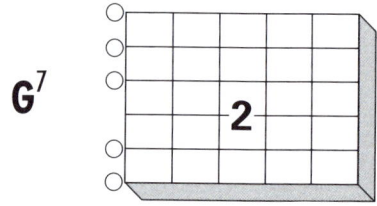

Em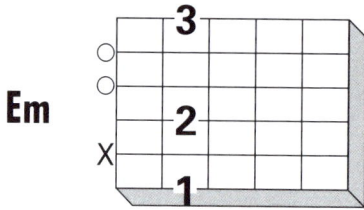

C⁹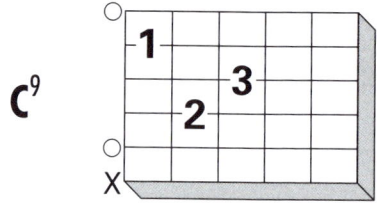

G⁷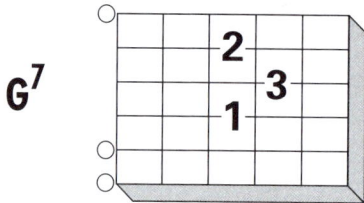

Bm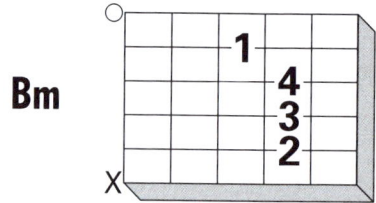

G^{6/9}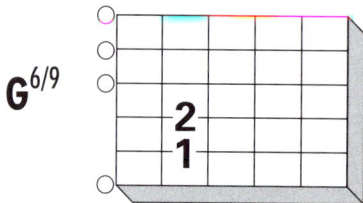

G^{sus4}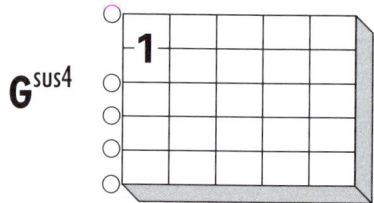

G⁷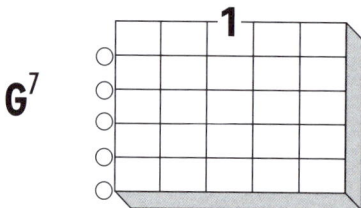

Bm⁷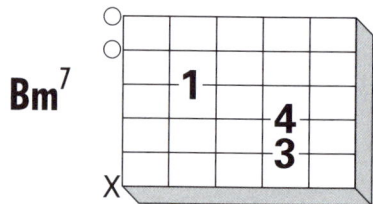

G Major scale

G Minor scale

G Major pentatonic

G Minor pentatonic

Open G2

This tuning has various names - occasionally it is referred to as Gadd9 or G9. Strictly speaking these names are not quite correct:

- the name Gadd9 indicates that the tuning has a third (B).

- the name G9 indicates there is a seventh (F).

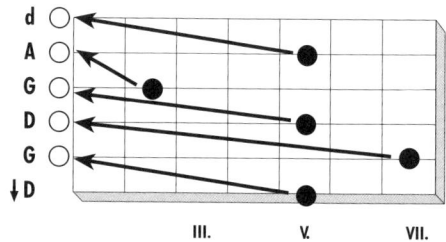

For this reason we have chosen the name Open G2, which admittedly is just as unfounded. No matter what name it has, it provides for some interesting tonal colors.

This tuning is rather striking due to the second interval between the G and B strings (similar to the D Modal, p. 38). Here, too, it is possible to play two consecutive tones of the scale without fretting one of them. The interesting sound effects resulting from this are similar to those in D Modal. Musicians influenced by traditional English and Celtic music also like to use Open G2.

In this tuning all harmonic effects sound especially good; above all the combination of fretted notes and natural (or artificial) harmonics creates countless fine-sounding chords ...

G
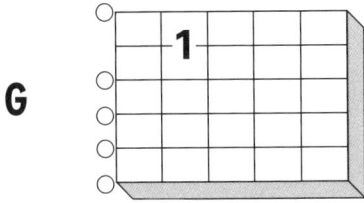

C
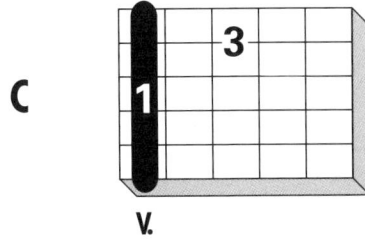
V.

Gmaj7
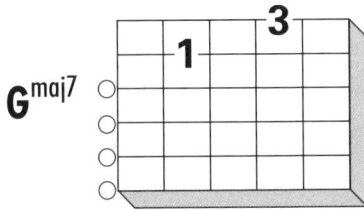

Gmaj7
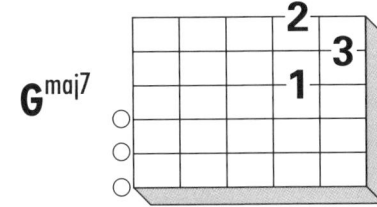

Dadd9
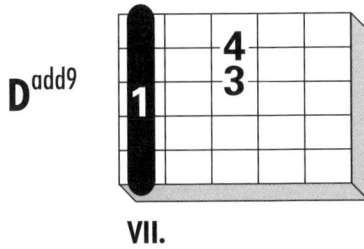
VII.

Am9
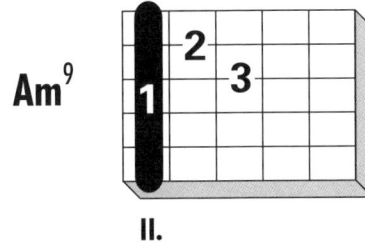
II.

G7
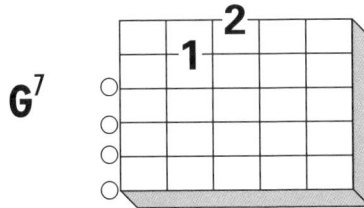

D
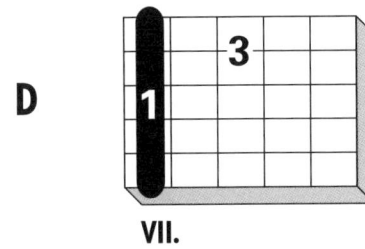
VII.

Gm
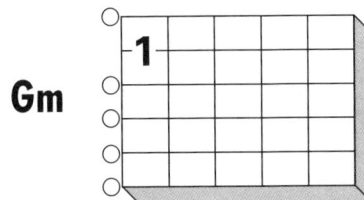

Gm9
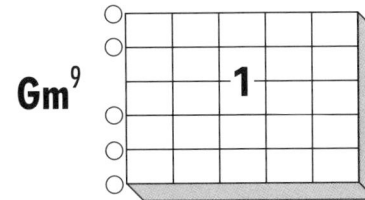

Gm^7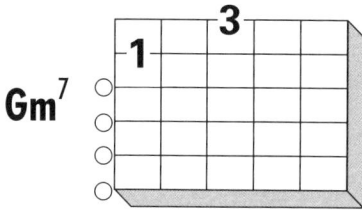

Gm^9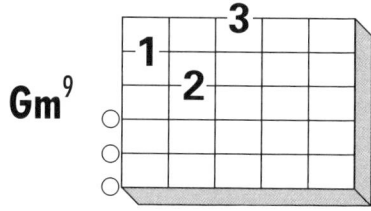

F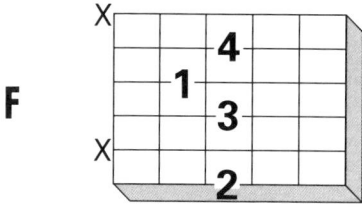

F^6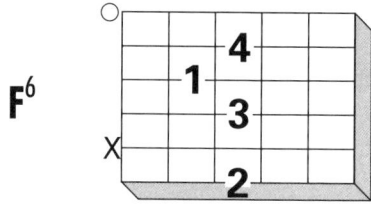

D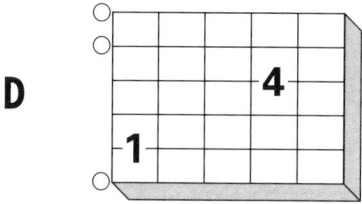

XI.

D^7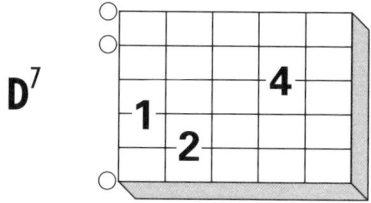

X.

B$\flat^6$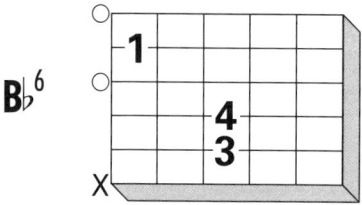

B$\flat^7$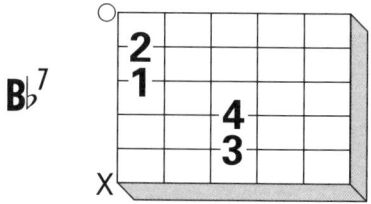

G^{maj7}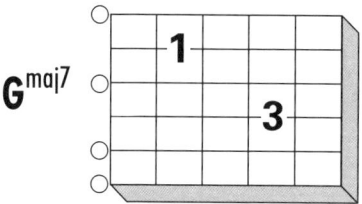

Gm^7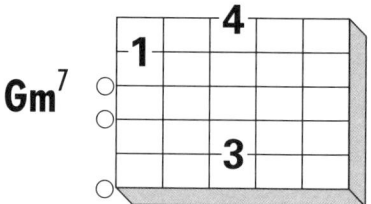

G Major scale

G Minor scale

G Major pentatonic

G Minor pentatonic

G sus4

This tuning is often referred to as **Sawmill.**

The term **sus4** stems from music theory and means the third of a chord is replaced by the fourth.

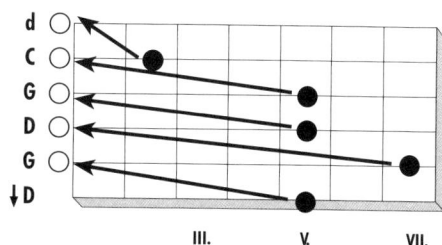

This is permanently the case in this tuning: the third note of the G Major scale (B) is replaced by the fourth (C). Gsus4 can also be thougt of as Open G tuning with the B string tuned up a halftone.

As Gsus4 has neither major nor minor character, it is particularly suitable for modal compositions or early (folk) music (which does not differentiate between the system of major and minor keys known today).

Eric Schoenberg and Martin Simpson are the best-known users of this tuning.

G
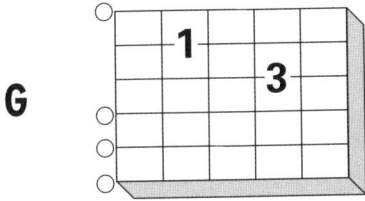

C
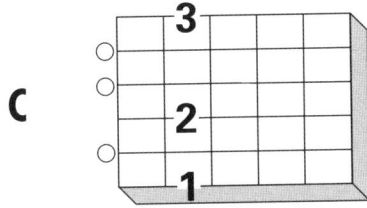

G^{maj7}
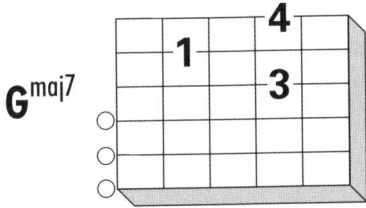

D⁷
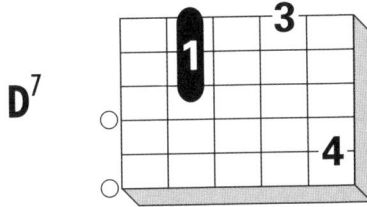

G⁷
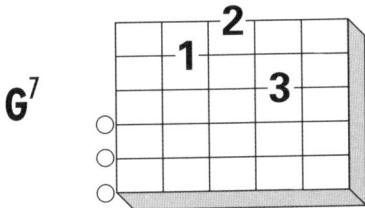

C
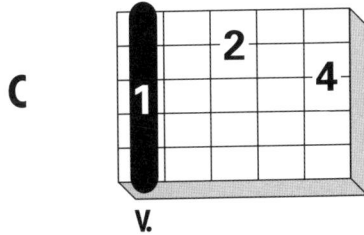

V.

C
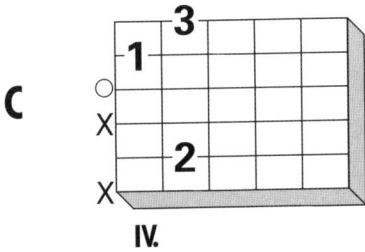

IV.

D
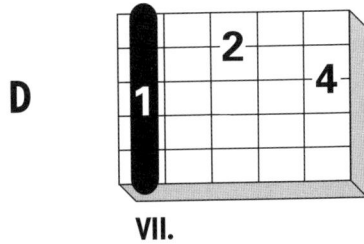

VII.

B♭ ^{add9}
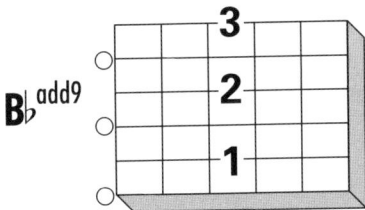

B♭
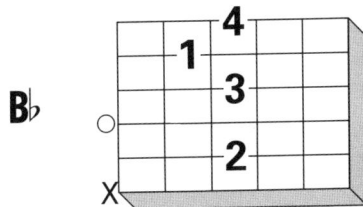

G sus4

Gmaj7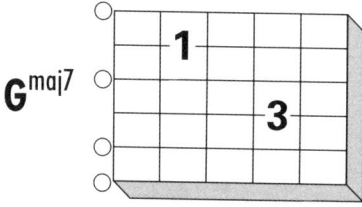

G6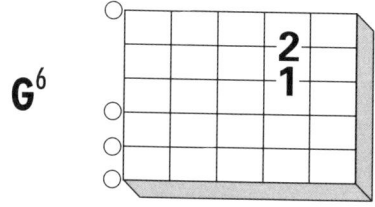

D7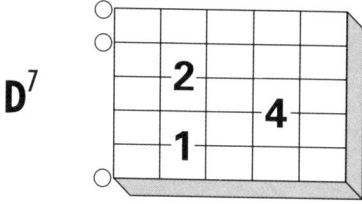

D7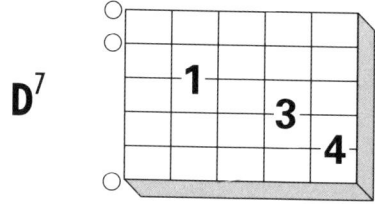

C7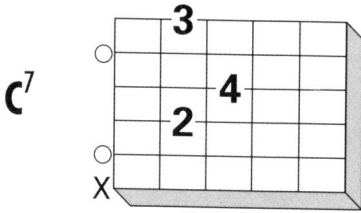

C6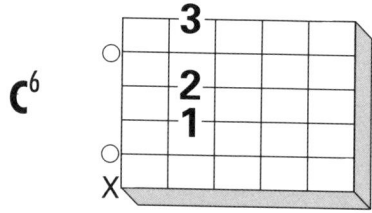

Gm7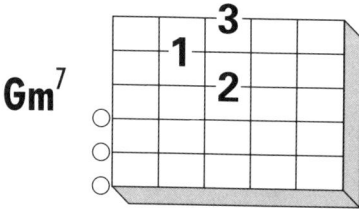

Cmaj7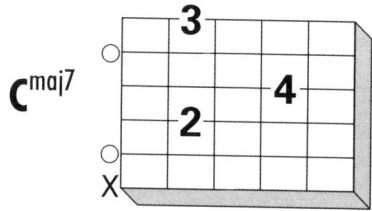

Gm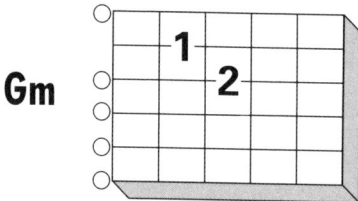

Gm11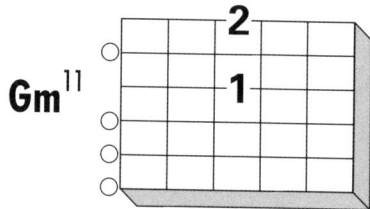

G Major scale

G Minor scale

G Major pentatonic

G Minor pentatonic

Open Gm

This tuning is the same as Open G except for one note. From Open G simply lower the B string a half-step.

Open Gm has the same advantages and disadvantages as Open G: As the lowest string is not the root, but the fifth of the scale, this tuning does not sound as full and sonorous as, for example, Open D. On the other hand, any number of minor chords can be performed in this tuning simply by playing a barre over all six strings, and in order to play any major chords, the second finger is placed on the fret above the barre on the B string. To turn the G minor chord, which the open strings would produce, into a G Major chord, only the B string on the first fret has to be fretted.

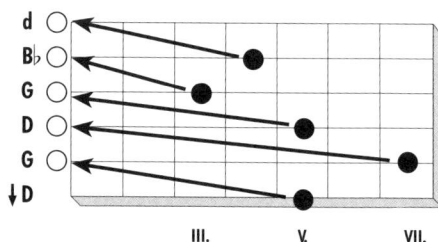

This makes Open Gm a very easy tuning when getting acquainted with open tunings, as a majority of the most important chords can be mastered within a few minutes.

Folk guitarists closely associated with Celtic and traditional English music like to use Open Gm. Stefan Grossmann, Peter Finger, John Renbourn and John Fahey (among others) use this tuning.

Gm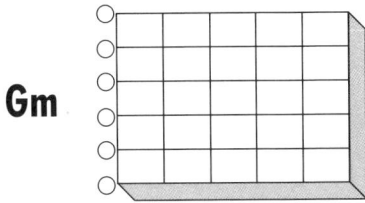

G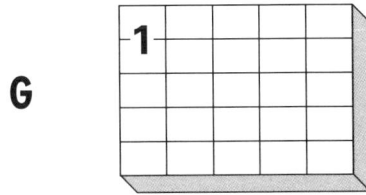

Gmaj7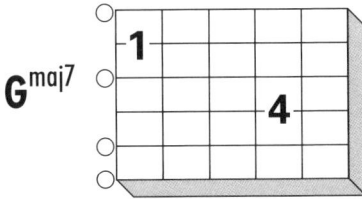

Gmaj7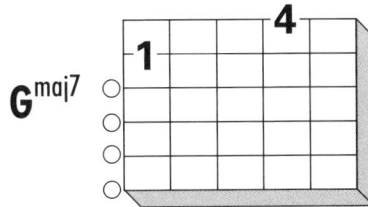

Gadd9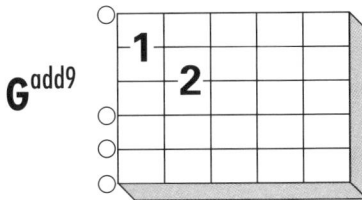

Cadd9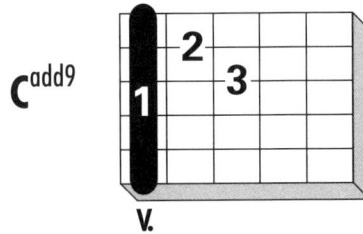

C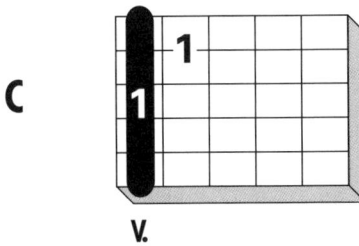

D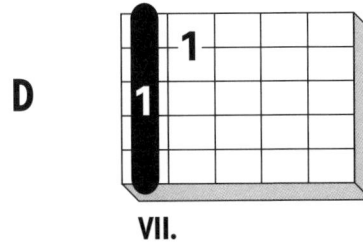

Gm11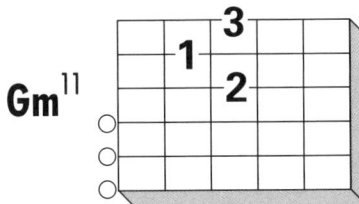

Cm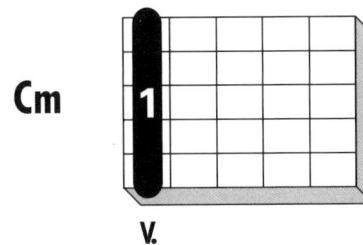

Open Gm

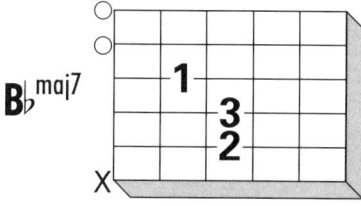

B♭maj7

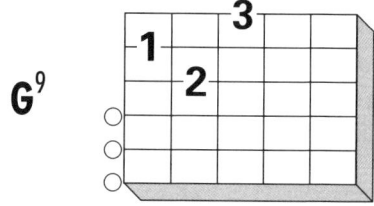

G9

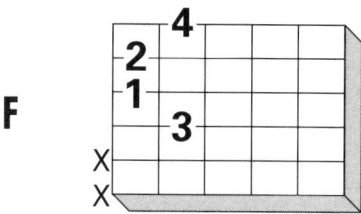

F

II.

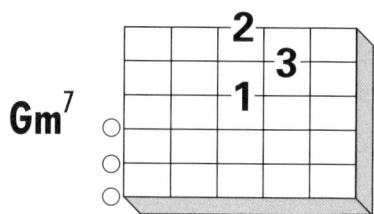

Gm7

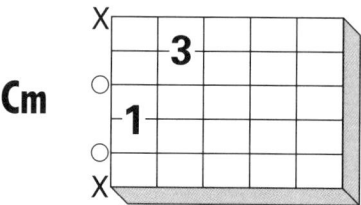

Cm

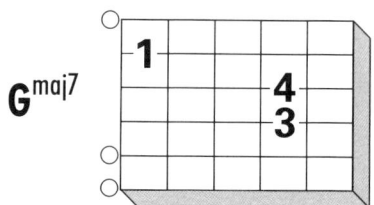

Gmaj7

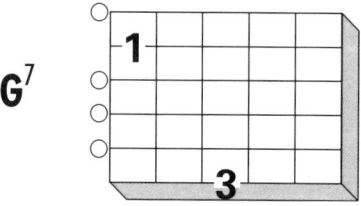

G7

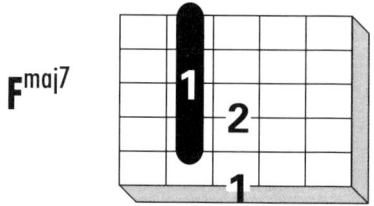

Fmaj7

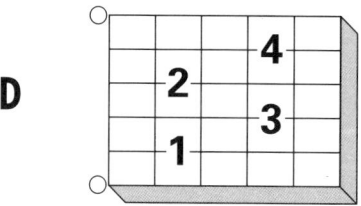

D

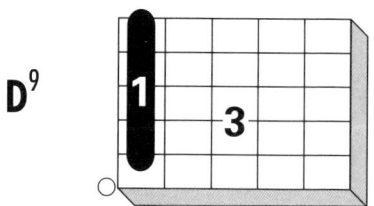

D9

II.

G Major scale

G Minor scale

G Major pentatonic

G Minor pentatonic

Open A

Open A is one of the tunings which sound particularly good on the guitar. It is relatively easy to find melodious voicings in this tuning. It is also excellent for rock music (like Open G as well), as even with strong distortion it does not sound discordant.

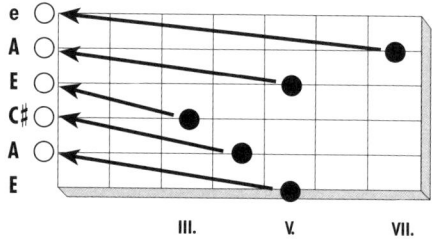

Natural and artificial harmonics sound particularly good in Open A and can be combined with fretted notes, resulting in attractive sound effects.

A variation of this tuning is E A D E A E. As this tuning is rarely used, we have dispensed with discussing it here in detail. It differs only slightly from Open A (the D string stays in standard tuning; is tuned therefore a half-step higher than in Open A). Nearly all chord-voicings, scales etc. can be taken from Open A, all tones on the D string are merely played a fret lower than in Open A.

Note:
There is another widespread variation on this tuning (E A E A C E), which is also referred to as Open A. This tuning is, however, merely a variation on Open G transposed up a whole-step, so that all chords and scales can be taken from Open G without any changes.

A
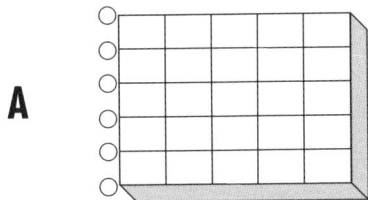

D
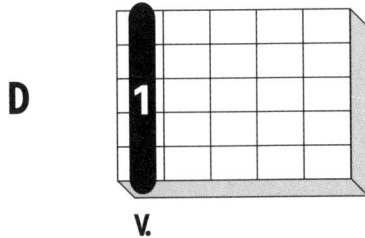
V.

F♯m
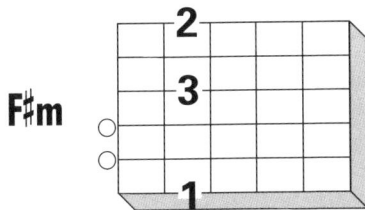

A⁷
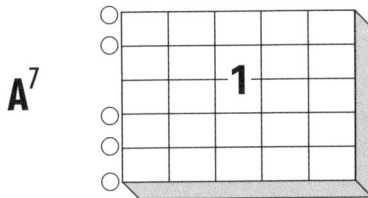

A^add9
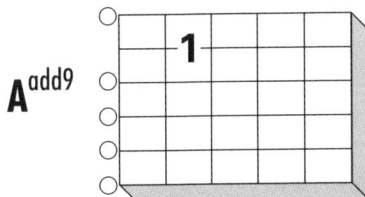

D^add9
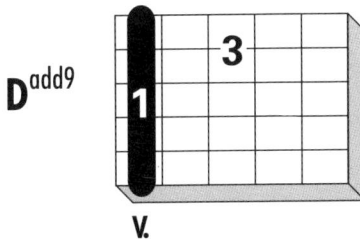
V.

E^add9
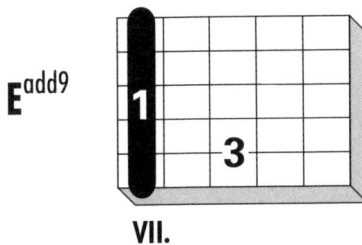
VII.

E
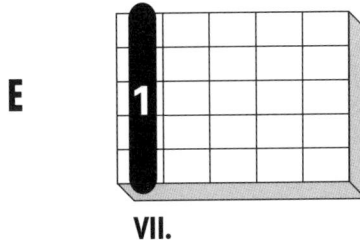
VII.

A⁶
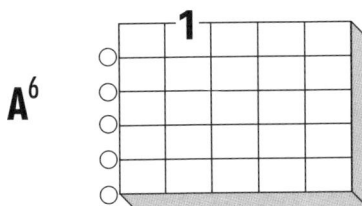

A^maj7
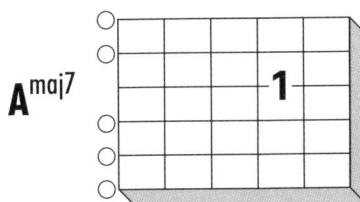

Open A

Am^6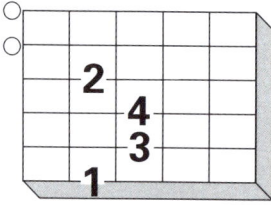

Em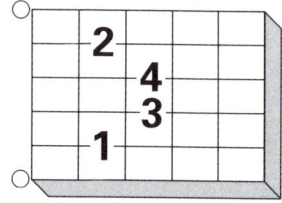

Am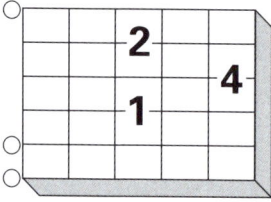

Am^7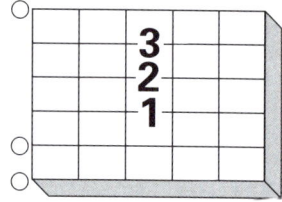

D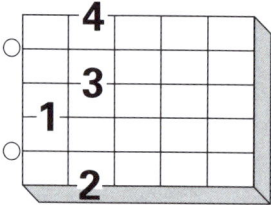

E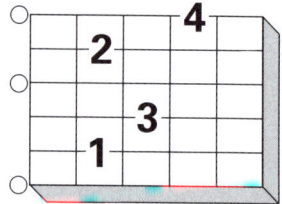

D^{add9}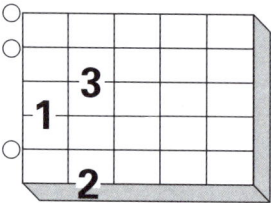

D^6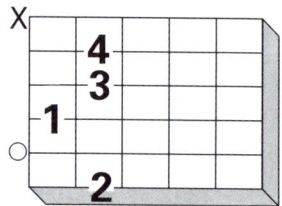

E^6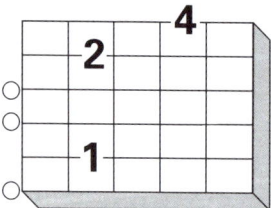

B^7

II.

A Major scale

A Minor scale

A Major pentatonic

A Minor pentatonic

Open C

This tuning is used very often on 12-string guitar, but also sounds excellent on standard guitar. Open C has been used by musicians such as Leo Kottke, Tracy Moore and John Fahey.

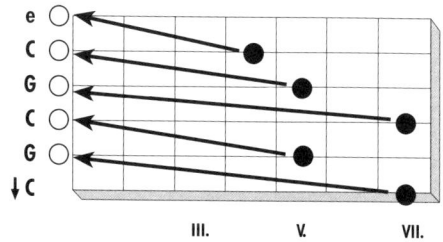

```
e  O
C  O
G  O
C  O
G  O
↓ C
```

III.   V.   VII.

This is one of the "lowest" tunings described in this book (with the exception of the B string). In order to avoid the bass strings in this tuning from vibrating in a completely uncontrolled manner, they should, if necessary, be replaced by a heavier gauge of strings. Open C sounds best on **Jumbo** or **Dreadnought guitars,** as through the large body the low frequencies are given particular emphasis.

One tuning closely related to Open C is C A C G C E. This tuning became popular chiefly through Jimmy Page of Led Zeppelin.

C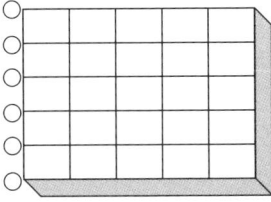

C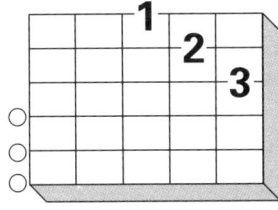

C^maj7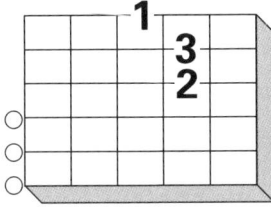

C^add9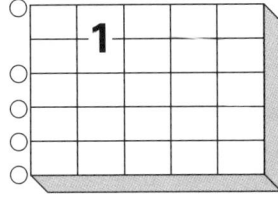

C^7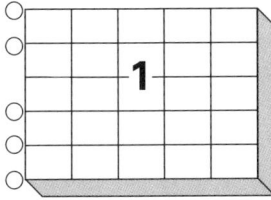

C^maj7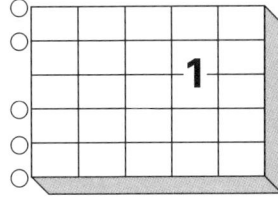

F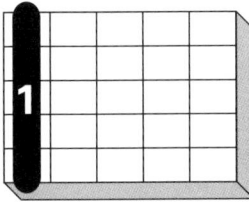

V.

G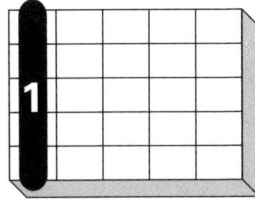

VII.

C^7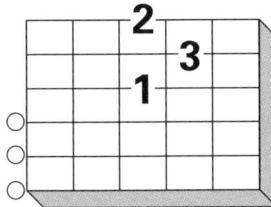

C^6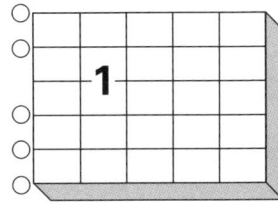

Open C

F^{add9}

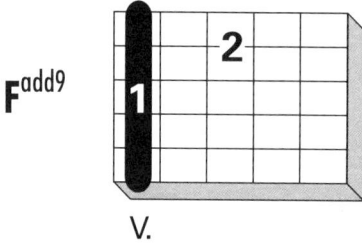

V.

C⁹

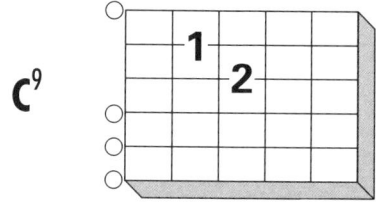

F⁷

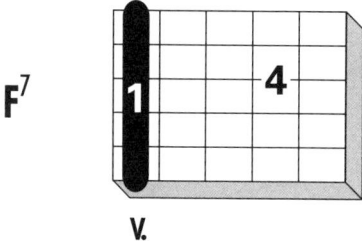

V.

G⁷

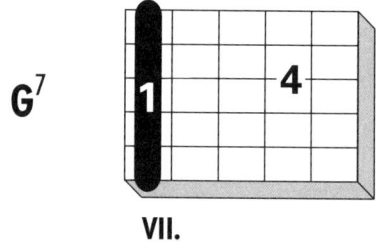

VII.

Am⁷

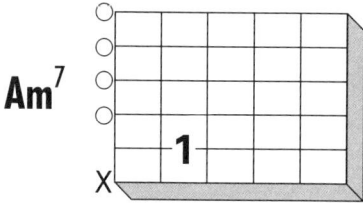

Am⁹

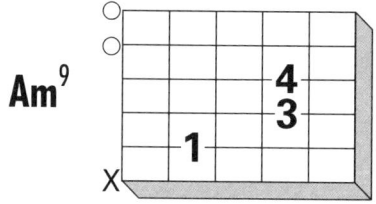

Dm⁷

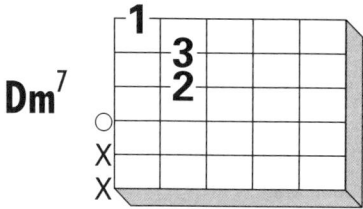

Em⁶

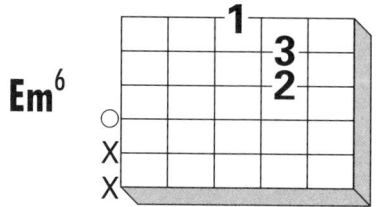

Cm

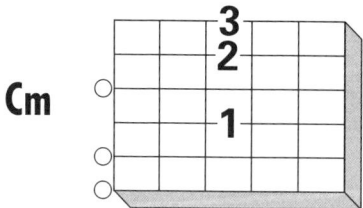

Dm

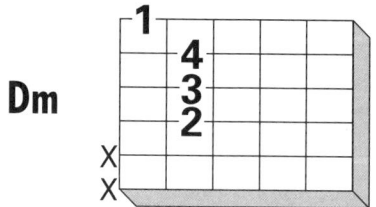

C Major scale

C Minor scale

C Major pentatonic

C Minor pentatonic

Open C2

This tuning is a little ambiguous and could just as well be listed under G tunings. In actual fact, Open C2 can be used both in C as well as in G. We have included it here under the C tunings on account of the lowest open string, but it could also be named Gadd4.

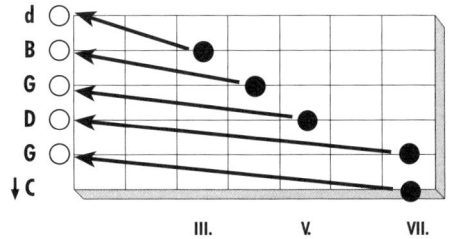

The low C gives this tuning a very special character and a resonance, which very few other open tunings produce.

Martin Simpson, Chris Proctor and Joni Mitchell use this tuning.

G

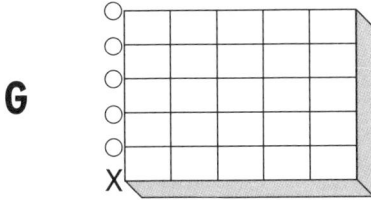

C

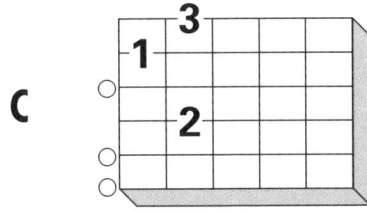

C^{maj7}

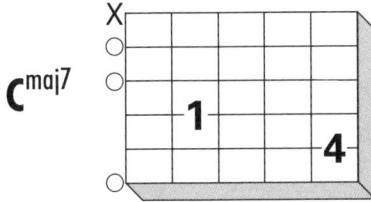

C^{add9}

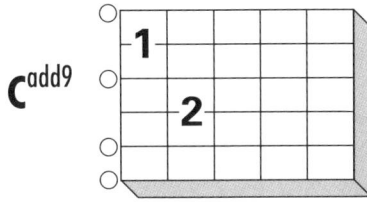

G^{maj7}

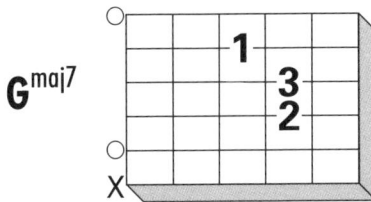

Bm

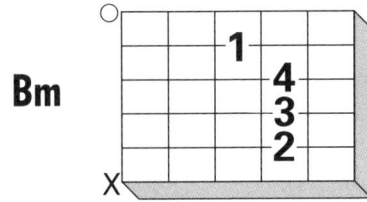

C

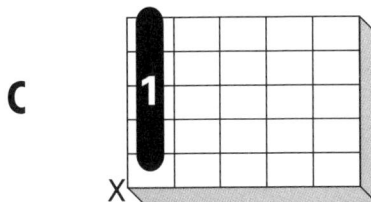

V.

D

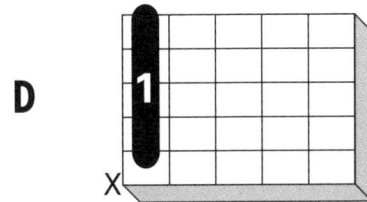

VII.

C$^{6/9}$

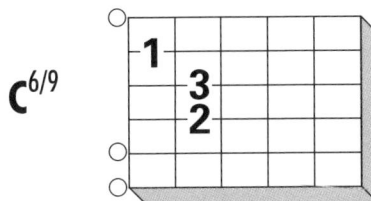

Am^{11}

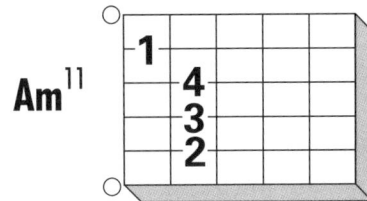

G

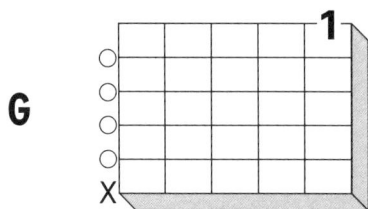

Bm⁷

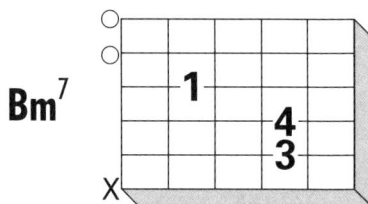

G⁷

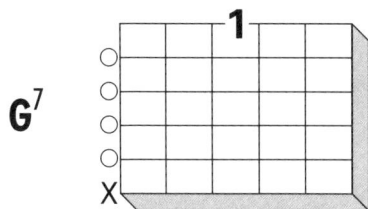

G⁷

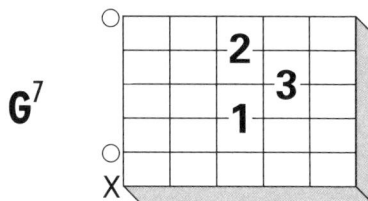

Gᵐᵃʲ⁷

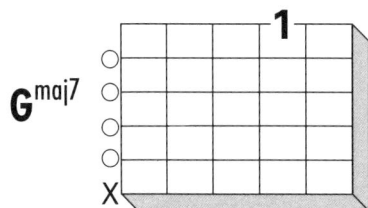

G⁶

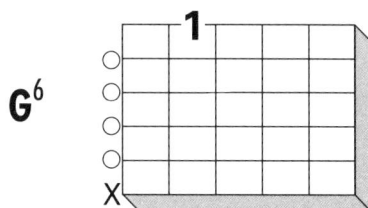

G⁷

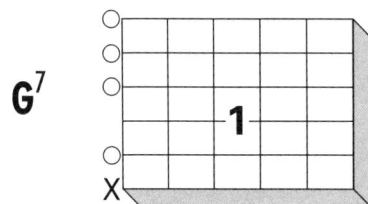

C⁹

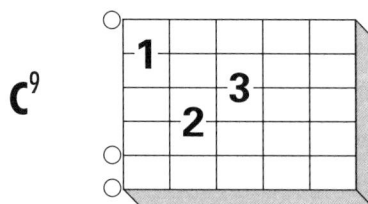

Cˢᵘˢ⁴

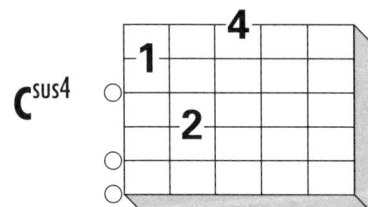

Cm

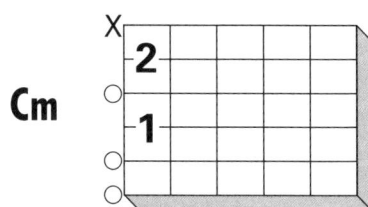

C Major scale

C Minor scale

C Major pentatonic

C Minor pentatonic

Open C3

C G D G B e

This nice tuning is suited especially to the key of C Major, not only on account of its low tonic on the open low E string, but also because the fifth – the most important note of the scale, apart from the tonic – is on the A string. Due to this, alternating bass techniques in this tuning are really easy to play.

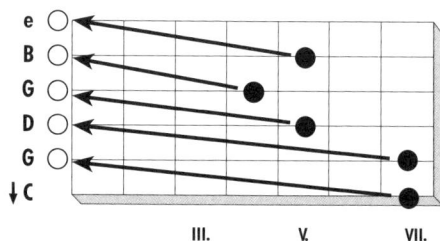

In addition, this tuning is relatively easy to tune and should not cause any major problems, even for the inexperienced.
For the advanced: the A string can be tuned an octave lower than the G string by ear. Then tune the low E string (7th fret) to the A string (now tuned to G) – done.

But Open C3 has yet another advantage: The four highest strings remain in standard tuning so that all chords played on these strings can also be used for Open C3. Even other chords can, with slight alterations, be adjusted to Open C3.
Players who have used this tuning include Preston Reed, Adrian Legg, Doyle Dykes and Chet Atkins.

C

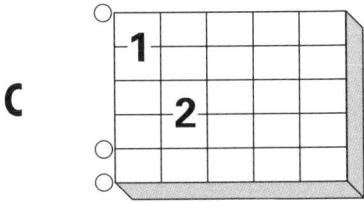

C

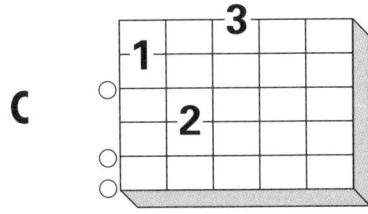

C^{maj7}

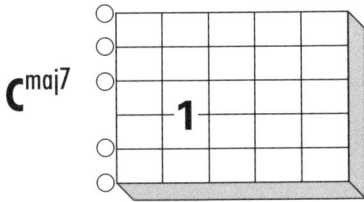

C^{sus4}

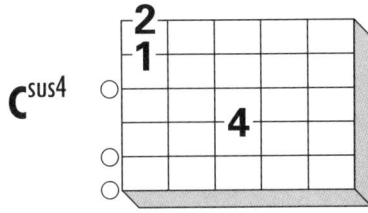

F^{maj7}

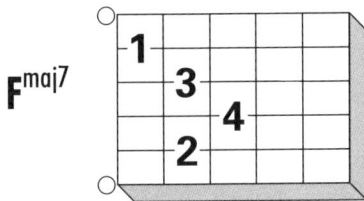

G^{7}

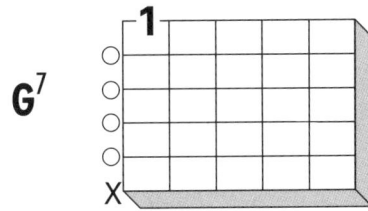

F

V.

G

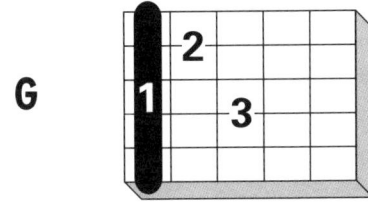

VII.

F^{add9}

V.

F^{maj7}

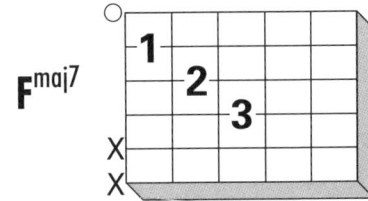

D^7

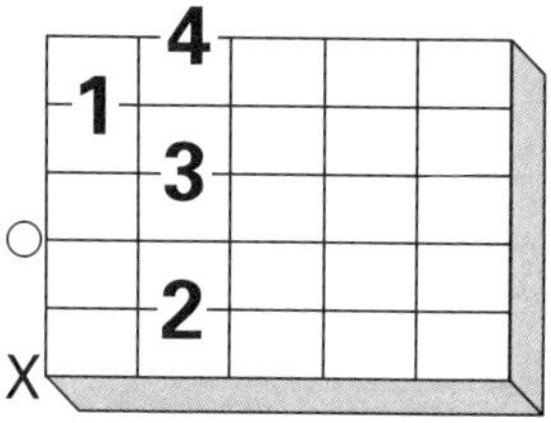

D

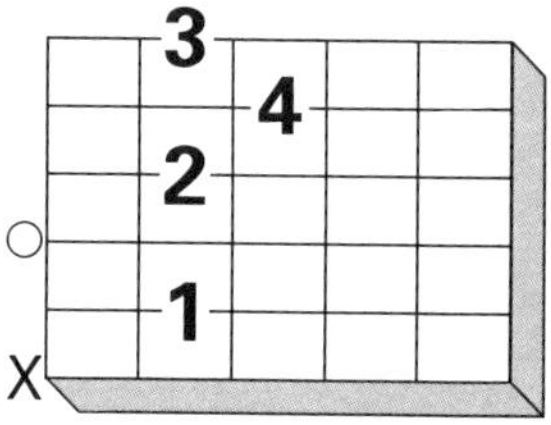

G

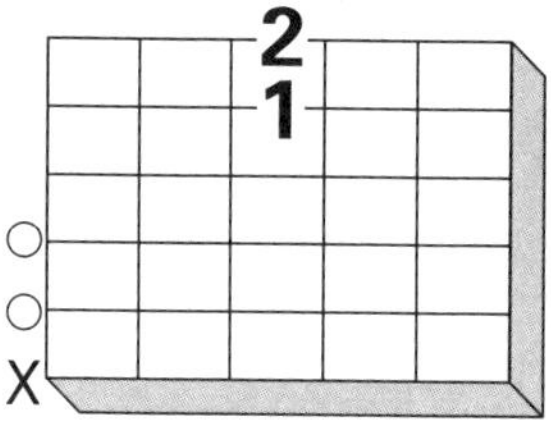

G^7

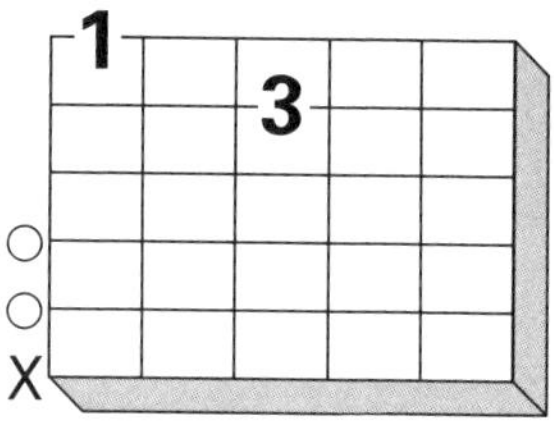

G^{maj7}

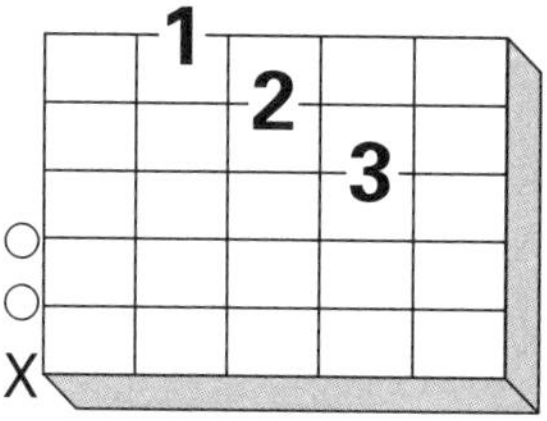

G

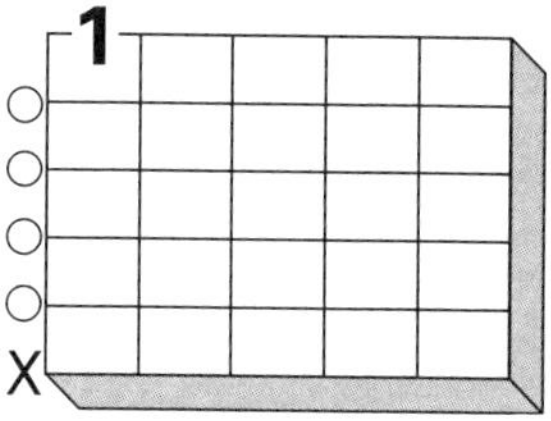

III.

D^{add9}

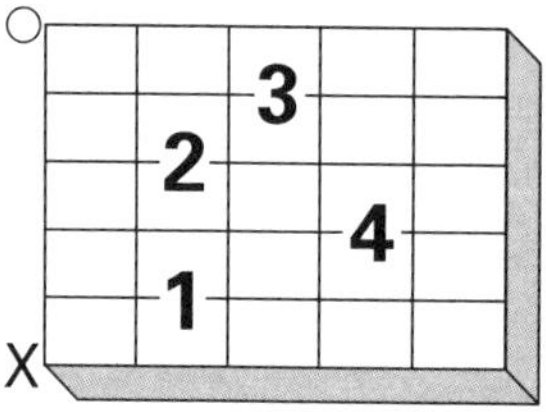

G^{add9}

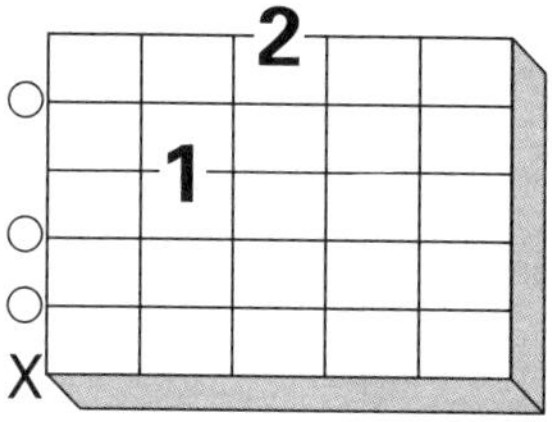

C

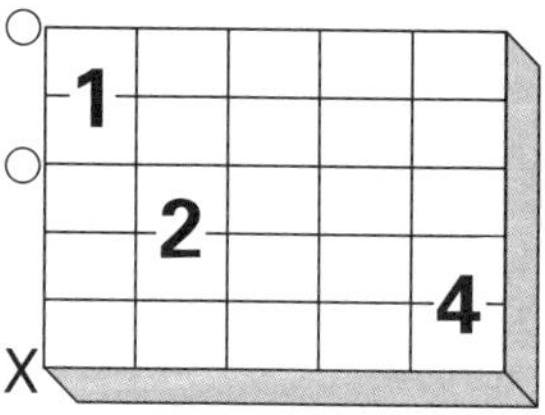

Em

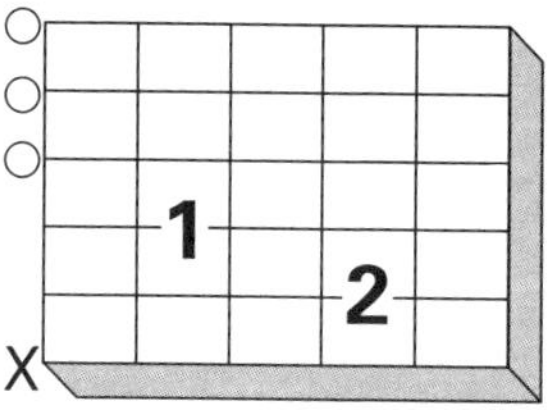

C Major scale

C Minor scale

C Major pentatonic

C Minor pentatonic

Open Cm

This is another variation on Open C. Starting from Open C, the high E string is tuned down a half-step to Eb, so that the open strings produce a complete C minor chord. This tuning has much in common with Open Gm and Open Dm, but sounds (as it is the lowest of these tunings) the fullest. Although Open Dm also has the tonic on the low E string, it is, however, a whole-step higher; whereas Open Gm has the fifth of the key as the lowest bass tone.

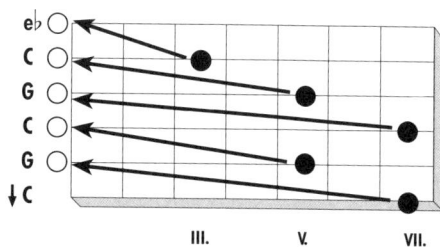

With the open E string, wonderful drone effects can be created; this tuning sounds best of all on a large-bodied steel-stringed guitar.

Cm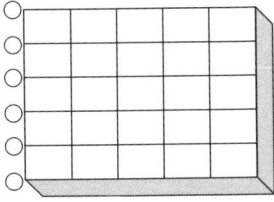

C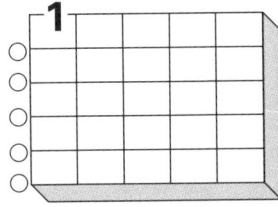

F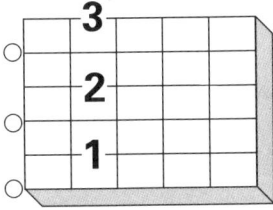

Cm⁹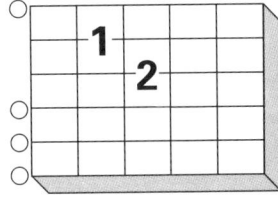

G^{maj7}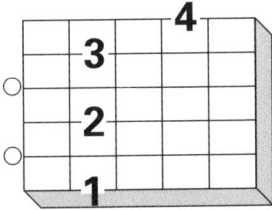

Cm⁷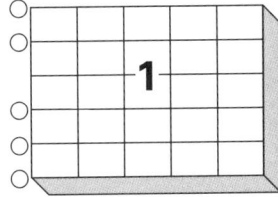

Fm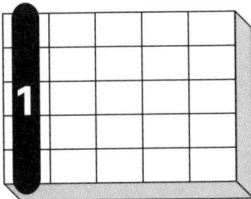

V.

Gm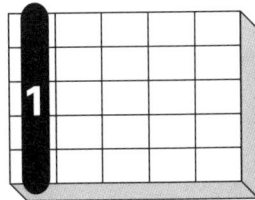

VII.

C⁷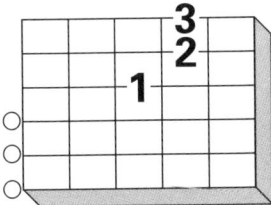

C⁷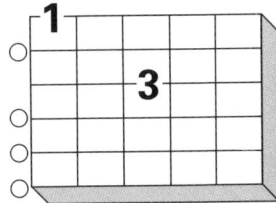

Open Cm

Dm

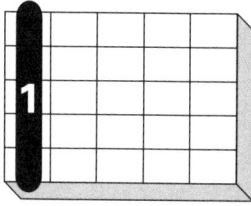

II.

F

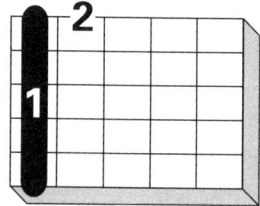

V.

Fmadd9

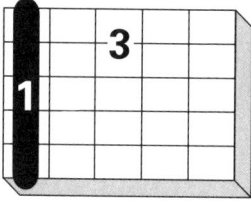

V.

Gadd9

VII.

Gmadd9

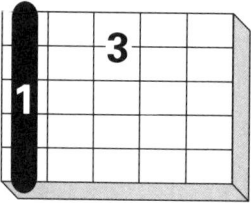

VII.

Fadd9

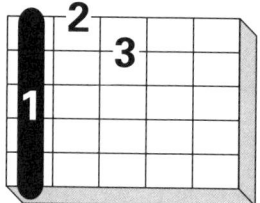

V.

B♭maj7

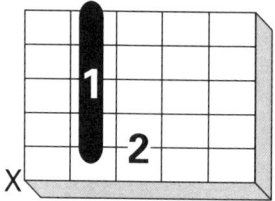

B♭

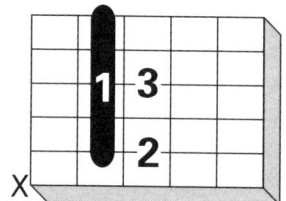

B♭add9

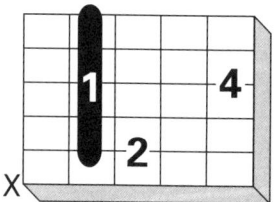

G

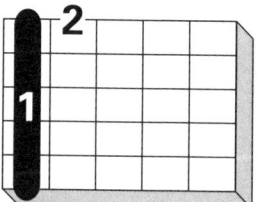

VII.

C Major scale

C Minor scale

C Major pentatonic

C Minor pentatonic

Lute Tuning

There are many different types of lutes, the styles of which vary as to the number of strings and tuning according to region and period. As in the case of early string instruments, the music was written down in tablature form; it was only later that its repertoire was transcribed to the musical standard notation commonly used today.

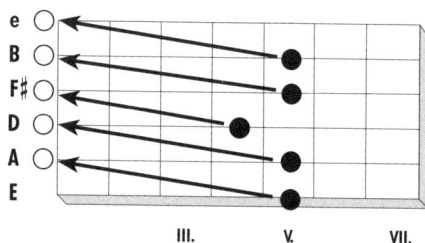

This is one of the most common lute tunings applied to the guitar.

This tuning is used chiefly to play lute music. Using this tuning, you can play directly from an (older) lute tablature. The only difference to the standard tuning of the guitar is the G string, which in lute tuning is tuned down a half-step to F♯.

This means that the chord voicings and scale fingerings of standard tuning can be used with only slight changes: all tones on the G string have to be played a half-step higher (one fret).

As the open strings already contain the most important notes of the D Major chord, this tuning sounds extremely good in the key of D Major.

G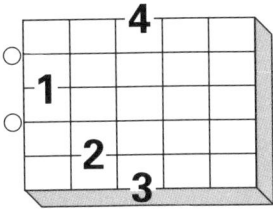

C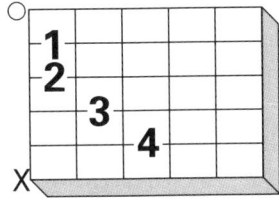

Gmaj7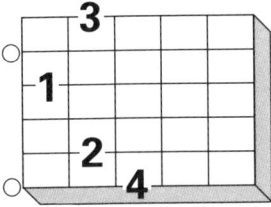

D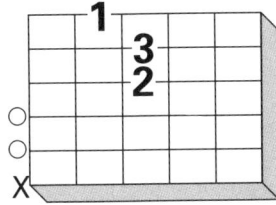

Dmaj7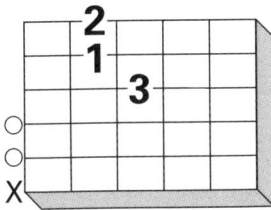

D7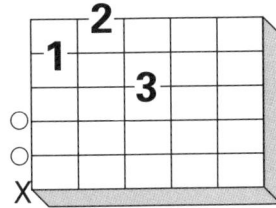

Am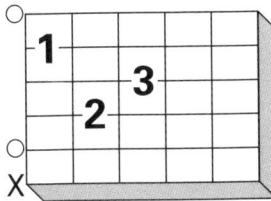

Dm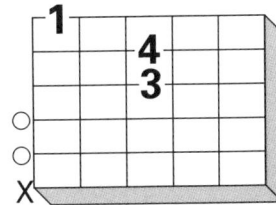

D6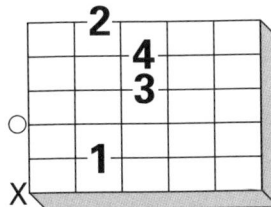

E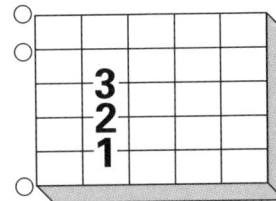

Lute Tuning

E⁷
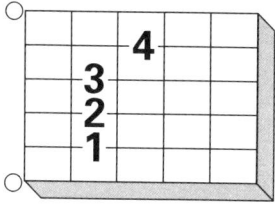

A
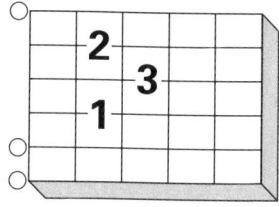

Em
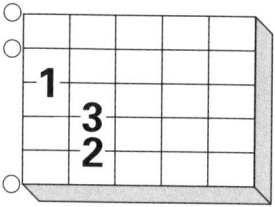

A⁷
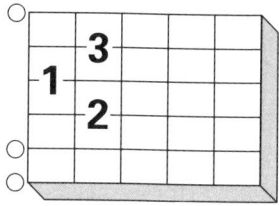

Aᵐᵃʲ⁷
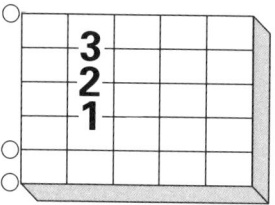

F
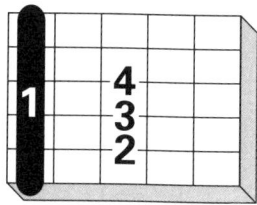

Bm
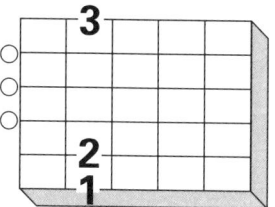

G
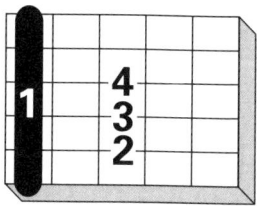

III.

Aˢᵘˢ⁴
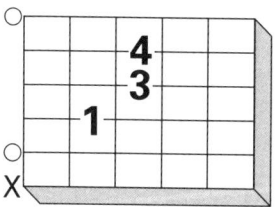

D
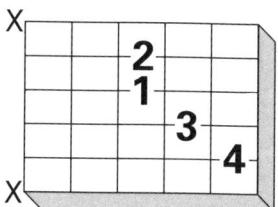

E Major scale

E Minor scale

E Major pentatonic

E Minor pentatonic

Tuning in Fourths

This is a relatively modern tuning. It evolved from a criticism of standard tuning which struck some musicians as being illogical: in standard tuning all strings are tuned in fourth intervals from each other, with the exception of the G and B strings, which are tuned to a major third. This results in the guitar not being completely balanced: all scale fingering and chords are played differently, according to which strings are being played. Fourth tuning overcomes this disadvantage. In fourth tuning, a chord played on the A, D and G strings, is simply played one (or two) string groups higher. It is true that this changes the **root** of the chord, but not the **type** of chord, which means that a major chord remains a major chord, a minor chord remains a minor chord, etc. The same procedure in standard tuning only works when all notes on the B string are adjusted accordingly while moving chords from one string group to another. The same also applies to scale fingerings: in standard tuning the fingering for a scale changes with each octave (if you want to stay in the same position), in fourth tuning the same fingering can be used for all octaves.

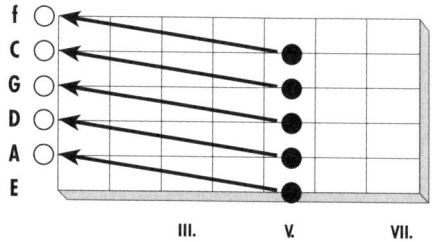

Here is an example: If you play an A Major scale, starting on the note A (5th fret of the low E string) over an octave (up to A on the 7th fret of the D string), the same fingering (or same pattern) can simply be started on the 7th fret of the A string to play the second octave:

The disadvantage of this tuning is that only a few chord voicings from standard tuning can be kept. This is, however, compensated for by the learning process for the most important types of chords and scale fingerings being dramatically sped up compared to standard tuning. Jazz guitarist Stanley Jordan plays in fourth tuning almost exclusively.

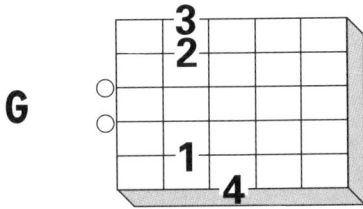

G

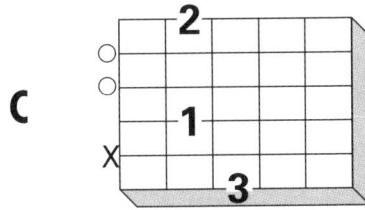

C

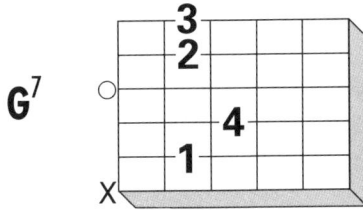

G⁷

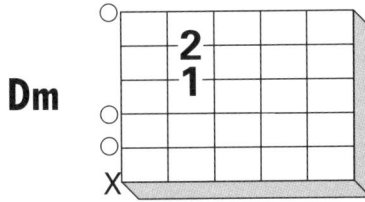

Dm

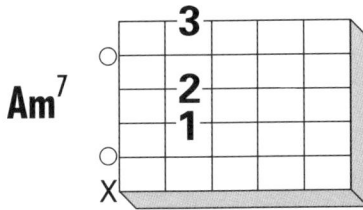

Am⁷

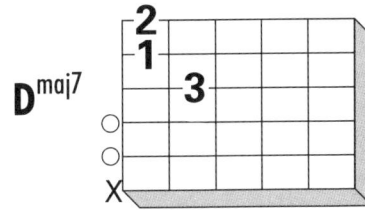

D^maj7

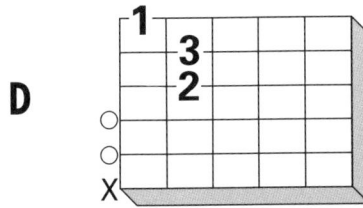

D

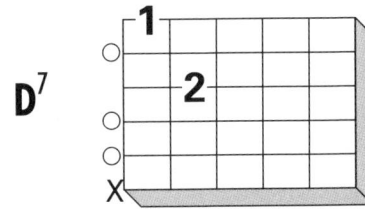

D⁷

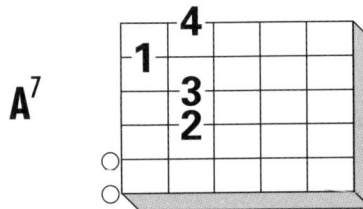

A⁷

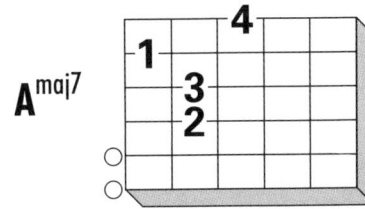

A^maj7

Tuning in Fourths

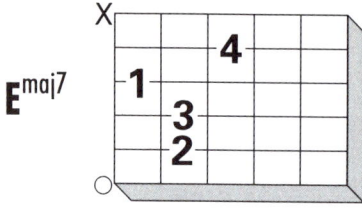

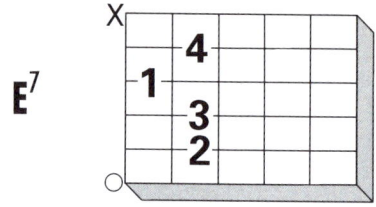

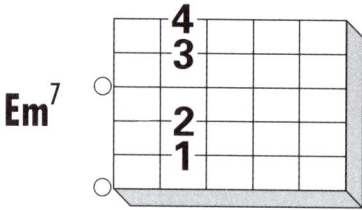

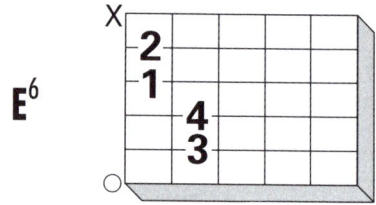

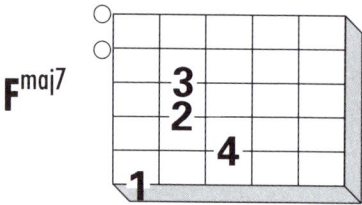

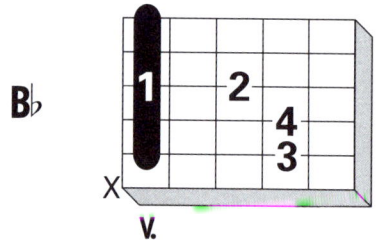

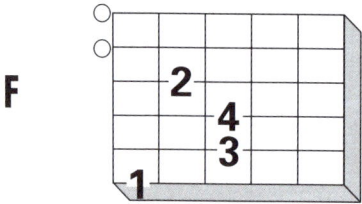

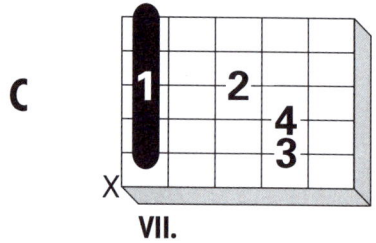

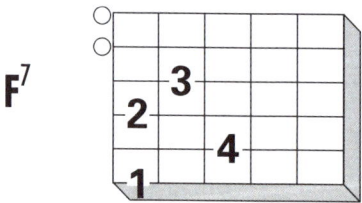

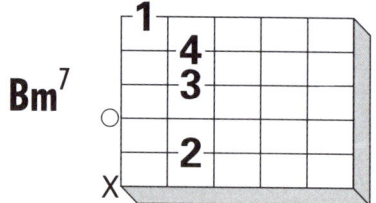

Emaj7

E7

Em7

E6

Fmaj7

B♭

V.

F

C

VII.

F7

Bm7

E Major scale

E Minor scale

E Major pentatonic

E Minor pentatonic

Special Forms of Tuning

Here we deal with some often used special forms of tuning.

All Strings Tuned To One Note

Guitarists with a leaning towards experimental playing, such as Adrian Belew, Buckethead or Robert Fripp, sometimes use this really exotic form of tuning. It creates a very interesting effect when, in the studio, a simple melody line is "doubled". The differing sound character of the individual strings produces a sound which requires a great deal of effort to imitate using traditional methods. This tuning is certainly an "experimental lesson". A well-known example is the song "Mind Riot" by Soundgarden; here all strings are tuned to E. A "variation" of this tuning is sometimes used by David Bowie, who plays a one-stringed guitar on stage.

Tuning Below Standard Tuning

Here, the whole guitar is simply tuned lower than standard tuning, mostly by a half-step to E♭ (E♭, A♭, D♭, G♭, B♭, E♭) or a whole-step to D (D G C F A D). Above all, guitarists belonging to the harder rock music scene like to tune guitars down by a quarter-step. The aim of all these moves is the same: to give the guitar an especially full, round and deep tone. This variant of retuning is often used with strings of a heavier gauge. Guitarists who often tune down are Edward van Halen, Yngwie Malmsteen and Ritchie Blackmore, to name a few.

Tuning the low E String lower

Heavy Metal and Grunge Guitarists in particular like to use this tuning trick. The debate as to how low the E string can be tuned is still in progress, but guitarists like Diamond Darrell (Pantera) have been seen to tune the E string down to C♯, and there seems to be no end in sight.
There is a mechanical appliance (Hipshot D Tuner) that, activated by a lever, tunes the low E string down to D and back and which has been used regularly for a few years by some guitarists, including Edward van Halen.

Appendix

Transposing and Capo tasto Tables

It very often happens that a song is written in a key which is either too high or too low for a particular singer (or that the chords stated are not known). There are two alternatives for guitarists to play the song in a different key:

1. By using a Capo tasto (in short "Capo")
2. By transposing into a different key

1. A Capo is an artificial saddle which can be fixed on any fret and "stops" all strings on this fret.

When playing with the capo, the chords change, as the capo has "moved" the nut. If, for example, a piece was played on the first fret with the chords C, F and G (that is in the key of C Major), and the same piece (using the same chord forms) is then played with a capo on the 4th fret, this produces the chords of E, A and B (that is, the key of E Major).

To use the capo there are two simple rules:

1. The new key always differs from the old one by the number of half-steps that the capo has been moved (counting from the nut).

2. When using the capo, the type and the structure of the chord stay the same, that means a minor chord remains a minor chord; a major chord remains a major chord etc.

The following table of notes on the fingerboard can be used as an assistance in locating the new keys:

e	F	F#	G	G#	A	A#	B	C	C#	D	D#	E
B	C	C#	D	D#	E	F	F#	G	G#	A	A#	B
G	G#	A	A#	B	C	C#	D	D#	E	F	F#	G
D	D#	E	F	F#	G	G#	A	A#	B	C	C#	D
A	A#	B	C	C#	D	D#	E	F	F#	G	G#	A
E	F	F#	G	G#	A	A#	B	C	C#	D	D#	E

Two more examples to practise:

a) A "standard" G Major chord with the capo at the 5th fret, turns into a C Major chord (five frets correspond to 5 half-steps steps; if you count five half-steps up from G, you reach C).

b) A "standard" A minor chord, with the capo on the 2nd fret, becomes a B minor chord (two frets correspond to 2 half-steps; if you count two half-steps up from A, you reach the note of B).

The capo has incidentally one more advantage: used skillfully, barre chords can be almost completely "avoided". The capo is seldom used above the 7th fret.

Transposing

The second way of playing a piece in another than the given key is by "transposing". This sounds considerably more difficult than it is. Using the chart, follow these instructions:

1. The initial chord is found in the first vertical column.
2. Look up the desired chord in the line attached to the right of this column.
3. In the column of this line the other new chords are to be found.

For this technique only the root of the chord is important, the type of the chord (major or minor) and additional notes such as the 7th or 9th stay the same.
From the 12th fret upwards, the notes repeat themselves.

CHORDS / FRETS	1.	2.	3.	4.	5.	6.	7.	8.	9.	10.	11.
C	C#/Db	D	D#/Eb	E	F	F#/Gb	G	G#/Ab	A	A#/Bb	B
C#/Db	D	D#/Eb	E	F	F#/Gb	G	G#/Ab	A	A#/Bb	B	C
D	D#/Eb	E	F	F#/Gb	G	G#/Ab	A	A#/Bb	B	C	C#/Db
D#/Eb	E	F	F#/Gb	G	G#/Ab	A	A#/Bb	B	C	C#/Db	D
E	F	F#/Gb	G	G#/Ab	A	A#/Bb	B	C	C#/Db	D	D#/Eb
F	F#/Gb	G	G#/Ab	A	A#/Bb	B	C	C#/Db	D	D#/Eb	E
F#/Gb	G	G#/Ab	A	A#/Bb	B	C	C#/Db	D	D#/Eb	E	F
G	G#/Ab	A	A#/Bb	B	C	C#/Db	D	D#/Eb	E	F	F#/Gb
G#/Ab	A	A#/Bb	B	C	C#/Db	D	D#/Eb	E	F	F#/Gb	G
A	A#/Bb	B	C	C#/Db	D	D#/Eb	E	F	F#/Gb	G	G#/Ab
A#/Bb	B	C	C#/Db	D	D#/Eb	E	F	F#/Gb	G	G#/Ab	A
B	C	C#/Db	D	D#/Eb	E	F	F#/Gb	G	G#/Ab	A	A#/Bb

Here is a small example to illustrate this procedure:

In a song the chords of C Major, F Major, D minor, A minor and G7 occur, indicating that the piece is written in C Major. Given these chords, the song is clearly too low for the singer. The suggestion is to try and play the piece in the key of G Major, so the C Major chord has to be transposed to G Major.

1.   The starting chord (C Major) is found in the first vertical column on the first line.
2.   The desired chord (G Major) is on the same line (i.e. the first) under the 7th fret (in column 7). All other chords required for transposing the piece are likewise to be found in this column.
3.   This system is now used for the other chords:
      The F Major chord is found in the first column (6th line). The corresponding chord in the 7th column is a C Major chord.
      The D minor chord is found in the first column (3rd line). The corresponding chord in the 7th column is an A minor chord, etc.

Using this system, the new (transposed) chords for this song are now:
G Major, C Major, A minor, E minor and D7.

This table can in fact also be used as a Capo table. Here the horizontal "fret"line shows the fret on which the Capo is to be placed, and in the vertical column belonging to it you´ll find the actually sounding chord.

Example:
You want to play this chord form of a G Major chord with the Capo placed on the 5th fret. In the first vertical column, the note of G is found in the 8th line, the entry in this line under the 5th fret is "C". Although the **chord form** you are playing is a G Major chord, the actually **sounding chord** is a C Major chord.

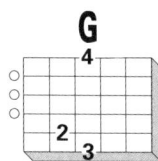

To gain a better understanding, we have described this procedure here in standard tuning; the procedure for each open tuning is principally the same ...

Again, the rule applies:
Only the root of the chord is important, additional notes of the chord such as the 7th, 9th or 11th stay the same.

Basic Chords
in Standard Tuning

Here we have put together the basic chords of the guitar (in standard tuning). The numbers at the side of the charts indicate the notes of the chords, i.e. the interval in relation to the root of the chord. Strings which are dampened or do not have to be played are marked with an "x", open strings with an "o".

All the fingerings shown are, of course, only suggestions and may be changed as required.

List of Chord Symbols

Symbol	Structure
Major	1 - 3 - 5
6	1 - 3 - 5 - 6
add9	1 - 3 - 5 - 9
6 / 9	1 - 3 - 5 - 6 - 9
sus2	1 - 2 - 5
sus4	1 - 4 - 5
maj7	1 - 3 - 5 - maj7
maj7 / ♯5	1 - 3 - ♯5 - maj7
maj7 / 9	1 - 3 - 5 - maj7 - 9
maj7 / ♯11	1 - 3 - maj7 - ♯11
maj7 / 13	1 - 3 - 5 - maj7 - 13
maj7 / 9 / 13	1 - 3 - 5 - maj7 - 9 - 13
minor	1 - ♭3 - 5
minor 6	1 - ♭3 - 5 - 6
minor 6 / 9	1 - ♭3 - 5 - 6 - 9
minor 7	1 - ♭3 - 5 - ♭7
minor 7 / ♭5	1 - ♭3 - ♭5 - ♭7
minor 7 / 9	1 - ♭3 - 5 - ♭7 - 9
minor maj7	1 - ♭3 - 5 - maj7
minor maj7 / 9	1 - ♭3 - 5 - maj7 - 9
minor add9	1 - ♭3 - 5 - 9
minor 7 / 11	1 - ♭3 - 5 - ♭7 - 11
minor 7 / 9 / 11	1 - ♭3 - 5 - ♭7 - 9 - 11
minor add11	1 - ♭3 - 5 - 11

7	1 - 3 - 5 - ♭7
7 sus4	1 - 4 - 5 - ♭7
7 / 9	1 - 3 - 5 - ♭7 - 9
7 / 9 / 13	1 - 3 - 5 - ♭7 - 9 - 13
7 / 9 / ♯11	1 - 3 - ♭7 - 9 - ♯11
7 / 9 / ♭13	1 - 3 - ♭7 - 9 - ♭13
7 / ♭9	1 - 3 - 5 - ♭7 - ♭9
7 / ♭9 / ♯11	1 - 3 - ♭9 - ♯11
7 / ♭9 / 13	1 - 3 - 5 - ♭7 - ♭9 - 13
7 / ♭9 / ♭13	1 - 3 - 5 - ♭7 - ♭9 - ♭13
7 / ♯9	1 - 3 - 5 - ♭7 - ♯9
7 / ♯9 / ♯11	1 - 3 - ♭7 - ♯9 - ♯11
7 / ♯9 / ♭13	1 - 3 - 5 - ♭7 - ♯9 - ♭13
7 / ♯11	1 - 3 - ♭7 - ♯11
7 / 13	1 - 3 - 5 - ♭7 - 13
7 / 13 / sus4	1 - 4 - 5 - ♭7 - 13
7 / ♭13	1 - 3 - 5 - ♭7 - ♭13
o7	1 - ♭3 - ♭5 - ♭♭7
+	1 - 3 - ♯5

minor	=	-, min.
maj7	=	Δ, Δ7, M, M7
o7	=	o, dim.
+	=	augm.

Although these chord symbols are the most commonly used, there are also other forms of abreviation, for example:

List of Chord/Scale Relationships

Chord	Scale

Major, 6, add9, 6/9.....Major scale (ionian)
Major Pentatonic

maj7...........................Major scale (ionian)
lydian

maj7/♯5.......................HM3 (harmon. Minor, 3. Mode)
ionian ♯5
lydian ♯5
augmented

maj7 / 9.....................Major scale (ionian)
lydian

maj7 / ♯11..................lydian
HM6
lydian ♯9

maj7 / 13...................Major scale (ionian)

minor ....Minor scale (aeolian)

minor 6 ....dorian
HM4
melodic Minor

minor 6 / 9 ....dorian
HM4

minor 7 ....Minor Pentatonic
aeolian
dorian
phrygian
HM4 (dorian ♯11)

minor 7 / ♭5 ....locrian
HM2

minor 7 / 9 ....aeolian
dorian
HM4

minor maj7 ....harmonic Minor
melodic Minor

minor maj7 / 9 ....harmonic Minor
melodic Minor

minor add9 ....Minor scale (äolisch)

minor 7 / 11 ....Minor Pentatonic
aeolian
dorian

7 ....Major Pentatonic (no 7)
mixolydian
HM5
Bluesscale

7 sus4 ....mixolydian

7 / 9 ....Major Pentatonic (no 7)
mixolydian

7 / ♭9 ....HM5
mixolydian ♭9
Halftone/Wholetone-Scale

7 / ♭9 / ♯11 ....mixolydian ♭9 / ♯11
Halftone/Wholetone-Scale

7 / ♭9 / ♭13 ....HM5

7 / ♯9 ....altered (melod. Minor asc., 7. Mode)

7 / ♯9 / ♭13 ....altered

7 / ♯11 ....mixolydian ♯11

7 / ♭13 ....Wholetone-Scale

o7 ....HM7
Wholetone/Halftone-Scale

+ MM3

List
of the most common Open Tunings

Open E .... E B E G# B E

Open Em .... E B E G B E

Open D .... D A D F# A D

Drop D .... D A D G B E

Drop D2 .... D A D E A D

Double-Drop D .... D A D G B D

Open Dm (Cross Note) .... D A D F A D

D-Modal (Dsus4) .... D A D G A D

Open G ....D G D G B D

Open G2 ....D G D G A D

Gsus4 (Saw Mill) ....D G D G C D

Open Gm (Saw Mill 2) ....D G D G Bb D

Open A ....E A C# E A E

Open C .... C G C G C E

Open C2 .... C G D G B D

Open C3 .... C G D G B E

Open Cm .... C G C G C Eb

Lute Tuning.. E A D F# B E

Tuning in Fourths .... E A D G C F